GW00359522

# Walks in Mysterious Hampshire

## Laurence Main

**Copyright** © Laurence Main, 1998

**All Rights Reserved.** No part of this publication may be reproduced, stored in a retrieval system, or transmitted in any form or by any means – electronic, mechanical, photocopying, recording, or otherwise – without prior written permission from the publisher.

**Published by** Sigma Leisure – an imprint of
Sigma Press, 1 South Oak Lane, Wilmslow, Cheshire SK9 6AR, England.

**British Library Cataloguing in Publication Data**
A CIP record for this book is available from the British Library.

**ISBN:** 1-85058-604-7

**Typesetting and Design by:** Sigma Press, Wilmslow, Cheshire.

**Cover photograph:** The ley going to Gallows Hill (Walk 17), *Laurence Main*

**Photographs:** the author

**Maps:** Morag Perrott

**Printed by:** MFP Design and Print

**Disclaimer:** the information in this book is given in good faith and is believed to be correct at the time of publication. No responsibility is accepted by either the author or publisher for errors or omissions, or for any loss or injury howsoever caused. Only you can judge your own fitness, competence and experience.

# Contents

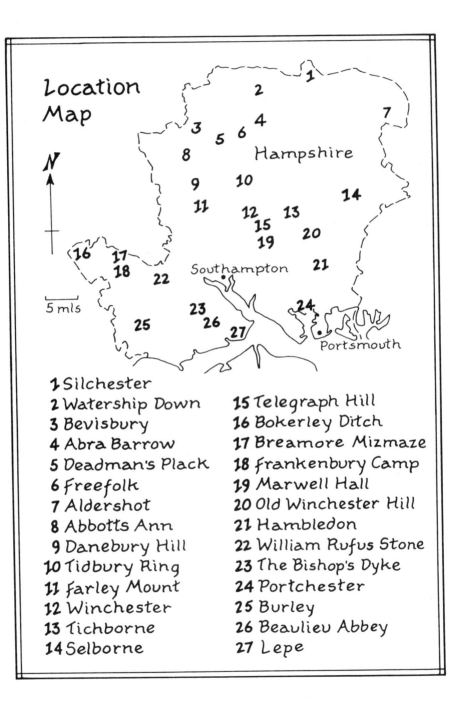

# Location Map

**N**

5 mls

Hampshire

Southampton

Portsmouth

1 Silchester
2 Watership Down
3 Bevisbury
4 Abra Barrow
5 Deadman's Plack
6 Freefolk
7 Aldershot
8 Abbotts Ann
9 Danebury Hill
10 Tidbury Ring
11 Farley Mount
12 Winchester
13 Tichborne
14 Selborne

15 Telegraph Hill
16 Bokerley Ditch
17 Breamore Mizmaze
18 Frankenbury Camp
19 Marwell Hall
20 Old Winchester Hill
21 Hambledon
22 William Rufus Stone
23 The Bishop's Dyke
24 Portchester
25 Burley
26 Beaulieu Abbey
27 Lepe

# Preface

This is a book of walks in Hampshire, averaging six miles in length, from and to places which represent the great store of legend, magic, mystery and sense of belonging to the living land that can still be perceived by the rambler. It has two aims. One is to open the eyes of the walker to the nature of the land he or she sets foot on, so that mutual love can be exchanged and humankind shakes itself awake to the need to live in harmony with Mother Earth. The other is to invite those armchair followers of the New Age fashion and even those most worthy souls who tend their organic or veganic gardens to embrace a little bit more of the planet, to let their soft feet inform remote areas that they are not neglected and to allow places where the spirit had survived more strongly to work through us.

The longest of these walks is ten miles, unless you extend Walk 10 to inspect Tidbury Ring, while there are no great hills to put off the faint-hearted. There is a wealth of wonderful scenery and the contrast with the noisy corridors containing the motorists is made clear. The motorcar is one of the chief enemies of the living earth and it makes a nonsense of your reverence for nature if you add to the pollution and demand for more roads. The local bus or train will be glad of your support. I relied on public transport to reach the starts of all these walks.

Having gained confidence by following routes from a book, go out and explore Hampshire on your own with the aid of those more precious keys to enjoying the countryside, the Ordnance Survey maps. The valuable 1:25 000 scale (2½" to one mile) Pathfinder maps are being replaced with Explorers.

*Laurence Main*

# Introduction

Escape from the towns and the busy roads and delve deep into the countryside of Hampshire and you may still be discovered by the spirit of the land. We do not possess this land; the land possesses us. There are sacred places, of spiritual importance and brimming over with memories of long ago, as John Masefield perceived 'the hillside thronged by souls unseen/Who know the interest in me, and were keen/That man alive should understand man dead'.

Stride along the prehistoric trackways of the Downs and patterns can be discerned in the landscape. Alignments of ancient sites, leys, linked with significant solar and lunar positions, can be observed. Danebury Hill seems to be a hub of these spokes, with satellite earthworks at places like Watership Down, of rabbit fame, and Abra Barrow. (You can learn more about leys by subscribing to The Ley Hunter: PO Box 258, Cheltenham, GL53 0HR.)

The landscape figure of a dragon, fire appearing to spout from its tongue, has also been identified at Chilcomb Ranges with its tail coiled around old Winchester Hill. Perhaps this dragon's cousin was killed at Burley Beacon, while the dragon-slayer Sir Bevis may be buried in the earthwork due north of Danebury Hill, guarding the border with Berkshire.

Dark deeds were done in the forests. The Rufus Stone may mark a willing royal sacrifice, while Deadman's Plack is where a scheming woman learnt to murder. Time stands still here and witchcraft thrives. When Hitler threatened to invade in 1940, the witches met to raise a cone of power in the New Forest. The effort was too much for three of them, who died on the spot. The survivors found their energy spent, but Hitler did not cross the Channel.

An invader did land near Lepe in the late fifth century, but Cerdic was only a leader of Saxons. He, himself, was British, so the Wessex dynasty he founded was British in origin. There is much evidence that Roman and post-Roman Britain was full of surprises. Carausius set himself up as Emperor of an independent Britain in the late third century. The massive walls of Portchester Castle perhaps protected his chief base. King Arthur's Sir Geraint may have been killed here and King Arthur himself is said to have been crowned at Silchester, while his Round Table can be seen at Winchester.

Walk the maze of life above Winchester and Breamore or make a wish at the stone above Selborne. Ghosts of monks may be seen here, as they often are at Beaulieu Abbey. Marwell Hall has its 'mistletoe bride'. There are no reports of ghostly cricketers at Hambledon but there should be. Visit the Bat and Ball Inn to discover why.

Neither is there a ghost of a crawling bishop at the Bishop's Dyke. Such crawling has to be taken seriously, however, as must the associated curses. When the Tichborne Dole was stopped, disaster befell the donating family. They should have learnt by suffering the drowning of an infant when they didn't give a gypsy food.

There must be a reason for Abbotts Ann's Virgins' Crowns, too. We could always try asking those modern phenomena 'the little green men' who are said to emerge from flying saucers. An angler at Aldershot could vouch for them. Perhaps they created the crop circles in the Devil's punchbowl – or perhaps they were created by mischievous 20th-century pranksters!

## The Ramblers' Association

Each walk in this book follows rights of way to which you, as a member of the public, have unrestricted access. Should you come across any problems, send full details (including grid references) to: The Ramblers' Association, 1/5 Wandsworth road, London SW8 2XX. Telephone 0171 582 6878. Better still, join the

Ramblers, go out on their group walks and volunteer to help deal with path problems yourself.

## The Country Code

- Guard against all risk of fire

- Fasten all gates (N.B. this is the official advice. In practice, farmers usually leave gates open on purpose, so that sheep can reach water etc., so 'leave gates as you find them')

- Keep dogs under proper control

- Avoid damaging fences, hedges and walls

- Keep to paths across farmland

- Leave no litter

- Safeguard water supplies

- Protect wildlife, wild plants and trees

- Go carefully on country roads

- Respect the life of the countryside

# 1. Silchester

*Route:*    Silchester – Museum – Benyon's Inclosure – Roman
            Wall – Amphitheatre – Roman Town – Museum –
            Silchester

*Distance:* 4 miles. Easy.

*Maps:*     O.S. Pathfinder 1188 Mortimer & Arborfield, O.S.
            Landranger 175 Reading & Windsor.

*Start:*    Calleva Arms, Silchester (SU 627621).

*Access:*   Bus no 143 runs to Silchester from Reading railway
            station. The nearest railway stations are at Mortimer
            and Bramley, on the line between Reading and
            Basingstoke.

According to Geoffrey of Monmouth, this 'woody place of the
Atrebates' was the site of King Arthur's coronation. A much more
likely spot, as Chris Barber points out in 'Journey to Avalon', is
Woodchester in Gloucestershire. There is an earlier reference to
Arthur being crowned by St Dyfrig at Caer Vudei (the camp in the
wood), which was the old name for Woodchester and was used
by Ambrosius as his headquarters. However, the broad acres of
this old Roman town are so impressive that it is easy to see why
Geoffrey should make it the scene of such a prestigious event.
Silchester also had a Christian church in Roman times, although
not on the site of the present church, which is dedicated to St
Mary and stands upon the site of pagan temples. There was a
town here before the Romans, The Atrebates were a Belgic tribe
who probably only preceded the Claudiuan invasion by 100

The Roman Walls, Silchester

years, coming from northern France. Their tribal chief Eppilus had coins minted in AD 5 bearing the letters Callev. King Cogidubnus dug defensive earthworks when the Romans invaded in AD 43. After the Romans abandoned Britain in AD 410, life continued here until well into the sixth century, when Arthur reigned.

## The Walk

**1.** With your back to the Calleva Arms, go right. Cross the road which is signposted for Reading on your left and go ahead along Whistle Lane. Turn left at its end to follow a lane to the Museum for Calleva Atrebatum, on your right. Continue to a T-junction.

**2.** Turn left along the road signposted for Tadley and Pamber Heath. Pass a house called Heatherbrae on your right and turn right along a forest track. Reach a cross tracks where the way ahead descends suddenly. Don't go down this!

3.  Turn right to follow the track to a fork, having passed through an old fort. Fork right and follow the track as it bears left through woodland to a road. Go right along the road for 200 metres.

4.  Look for a public footpath signpost on your right which points across the road, to your left. Turn left to take this path, which descends into woodland, then climb up to a stile in the perimeter fence on your right. Cross it and continue through a field to take another stile in the hedge opposite. Turn right along a bridle-way and go left at a lane to follow it past the walls of the Roman town, on your right.

5.  Look for a stile on your right which gives access to the Roman walls. Then divert over a stile on your left to see the remains of the amphitheatre. Turn right with the road to reach St Mary's church, on your right.

6.  Take the path through the churchyard, passing the church on your left. Bear right past a barn on your right and go left to follow a track through the interior of Calleva Atrebatum to an earthen bank at the western end. Turn left to walk with the earthwork on your right.

7.  Turn right along a path out of the Roman town and soon bearing left back to its museum. Turn left along the lane to retrace your steps to Whistle Lane, where you go right to return to the bus stop outside the Calleva Arms.

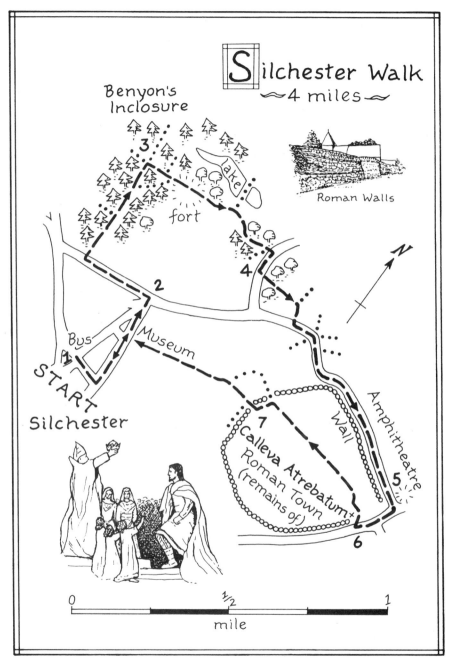

Silchester Walk
~4 miles~

Benyon's Inclosure

Roman Walls

Lake

fort

3

2

4

Bus

Museum

START

Silchester

7

Calleva Atrebatum
Roman Town
(remains of)

Wall

Amphitheatre

5

6

N

0     ½     1
mile

# 2. Watership Down

***Route:***     Kingsclere – Watership Down – Ladle Hill –
            Ecchinswell – Kingsclere

***Distance:*** 9½ miles. Strenuous.

***Maps:***      O.S. Pathfinder 1203 Kingsclere, O.S. Landranger 174
            Newbury & Wantage.

***Start:***     Bus shelter, The Square, Kingsclere (SU 526587).

***Access:***    Buses nos 32 and 32A run to Kingsclere from
            Basingstoke and Newbury.

## Rabbits and the Moon

Watership Down has become internationally famous for its rab-
bits, the heroes of Richard Adams' book 'Watership Down'. Perhaps there is a special link between out fertile friends and the
moon. The tumuli on Watership Down mark the point on the horizon where the most northerly moon-rise as seen from the significant spot of Danebury Hill (Walk 9) occurs. Looking back
down this line to Danebury, it includes a large tumulus and a dew
pond at Angledown. With a bearing of about 40 degrees, this
alignment is known as the northerly major standstill. What the
sun does in one year, the moon does in a month. This lunation period of 29.5 days completes the cycle from new moon to full moon
and back to new moon again. The moon has another rhythm, averaging 27.32 days and known as the lunar orbital period. This is
the time taken between the moon's passage past a fixed star. The
two periods differ by about 2.2 days because while the moon is
orbiting the earth, so is the earth orbiting the sun and it takes an

extra couple of days for the moon to line up with the earth and the sun. The moon-rise and moon-set directions swing in two arcs, respectively, from a northerly point (or standstill) to a southerly point (or standstill). The swing of this arc varies from a maximum (major) angle to a minimum (minor) one. It takes that arc 9.3 years to change from a major standstill swing to a minor one, or 18.6 years to complete a full cycle. The attempt to integrate the moon with the sun within an effective calendar was important to our ancestors, as indicated by the Aubrey Circle at Stonehenge. The ancients valued the achieving of harmony between sun and moon, male and female. Recommended reading on this subject is 'A Key to Stonehenge' by Robin Heath.

It's worthwhile taking a look at the fort on Ladle Hill. This is remarkable for being half-completed, thus giving an insight into construction methods. It's as if defences had to be dug and erected in haste, then trouble blew over, leaving gaps in the earthworks and piles of materials. Could the name be linked somehow to Ceridwen's Cauldron?

## The Walk

**1.** From the bus shelter in Kingsclere, go left along Swan Street, passing St Mary's church on your right. Bear right at a fork to take the road signposted for Sydmonton. Pass a hedged track on your left, then a gated farm access lane on your left. Reach another gate on your left.

**2.** Turn left through this gate to go ahead beside a hedge on your left and towards the Downs. Fork left at a waymark post bearing a yellow arrow and take a grassy path between fields. Turn right along a track which runs uphill beside a hedge on your right. Ignore the first track into a patch of woodland on your left.

**3.** Turn left in the corner waymarked by a yellow arrow. Climb the wooded slope to cross a stile in the top fence and bear right uphill. Walk along the crest of the hill with a fence on your left and go ahead over a stile beside a signpost. Bear left across training gallops where signposted and continue through a small gate. Go right along a ridgeway track. Reach a tumulus in an open space on your left, while the second tumulus is covered by trees and brambles on your left.

4. Bear right to pass the summit trig. point on your left and take the Wayfarer's Walk, waymarked by a distinctive green arrow, ahead. Bear left through a small gate, continue to cross a lane and go along a firm track.

5. Take the waymarked gate into the Sydmonton Court Estate and follow the waymarked route which follows a fence on your left and bears left through a gate, go left for 250 metres, then turn right with a track through a field and pass tumuli on your left. Reach the ramparts of the pre-historic fort on Ladle Hill on your right.

6. Bear left, as waymarked, away from the hill fort. After 400 metres reach a path junction waymarked by a cairn of stones and turn sharply right, away from the Wayfarer's Walk. Continue through a gate waymarked for the Off Road Cycle Trail and eventually reach a road junction.

7. Take the road ahead, as signposted for Burghclere, immediately passing the gated drive for Sydmonton Court on your right (this is the country home of composer Sir Andrew Lloyd Webber). Pass farm buildings on your right and turn right along a signposted footpath which is a track. Bear left along another track when it comes in sharply from your right. Follow it around a bend on your left. Turn right at a junction to follow the track past Watership Farm.

8. Go left along a road into Ecchinswell. Pass the Royal Oak pub on your right, then the road signposted for Kingsclere. Turn right down a No Through Road. At the end of this, turn left along a signposted and enclosed footpath.

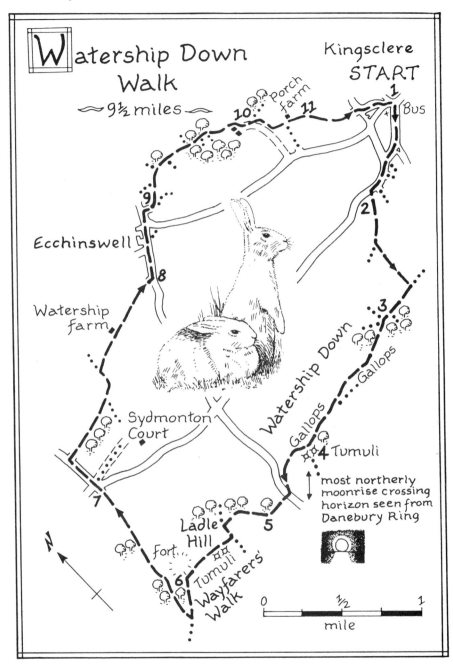

Watership Down Walk
~ 9½ miles ~

Kingsclere
START

1
Bus

10   Porch farm   11

9

Ecchinswell

8

Watership farm

2

3

Watership Down

Gallops

Gallops

Gallops

4 Tumuli

most northerly
moonrise crossing
horizon seen from
Danebury Ring

Sydmonton
Court

7

5

Ladle
Hill

Fort

6   Tumuli   Wayfarers' Walk

N

0        ½        1
mile

**9.** Emerge over a stile in a corner of a field. Walk beside the hedge on your left. Ignore a stile and a footbridge on your left. Go ahead to cross the stile in the corner and pass a bridge over a stream on your left. Continue along a hedged path, then go ahead through woodland at a signposted path junction. Emerge to cross a footbridge in the corner and go ahead past another footbridge for a waymarked path on your left. Bear right with a bridleway (blue arrow) to pass farm buildings on your right.

**10.** Turn left along a lane for 100 metres, then fork left along a bridleway. Go right at a junction to take a hedged path for 300 metres. Turn left over a stile and walk beside a hedge on your left. Turn right at a farm for 50 metres along a track to a gate. Turn left over a stile to pass the farm on your left and continue under power lines.

**11.** Go ahead through a gate in the corner to bear slightly right through the next field to a stile in a corner. Cross it and follow an enclosed path (Frogs Hole) to a road. Go right to a junction and turn left to return to the bus shelter in Kingsclere.

# 3. Bevisbury

**Route:**   Enham Alamein – Bevisbury – Tangley – Hatherden – Enham Alamein

**Distance:** 10 miles. Moderate.

**Maps:**   O.S. Pathfinders 1202 Ludgershall & Hurstbourne Tarrant and 1222 Andover, O.S. Landranger 185 Winchester & Basingstoke.

**Start:**   The Institute, Enham Alamein (SU 367491).

**Access:**  Buses nos 60 and 61 run to Enham Alamein from Winchester, Andover (the nearest railway station) and Newbury.

## Bevisbury

The ancient earthwork in the shape of a ring near the border between Hampshire and Berkshire and aligned with the Roman road from Winchester (which may follow a ley) is associated with a great hero of fourteenth century romance, Sir Bevis. It may even be his grave. It is probably a significantly spiritual spot, lying on a line drawn going north from Mottisfont Abbey through that tumulus at the eastern end of Danebury Hill which is the focus of attention for so many other alignments of sacred sites.

Bevis was the son of Sir Guy of Hampton (now Southampton) and the daughter of the King of Scotland. Bevis' mother had a lover with whom she connived to murder Sir Guy. Bevis was then sent to be sold as a slave to the Moslems. The Paynim king's daughter, Joisyan, fell in love with him and after exciting adventures, including fighting a dragon, the couple escaped to England.

On the way, Bevis had to fight a giant who, upon his defeat, sub-
mitted to Bevis and became his loyal servant. Bevis returned to
Hampton and boiled his mother's lover into dog's meat in a great
cauldron. His mother jumped to her death from the top of a high
tower. The people hailed Bevis as their deliverer. Eventually, after many more adventures, Bevis, Joisyan and Bevis' great horse,
Arundel (meaning Swallow), all died within moments of each
other. John Bunyan and Samuel Pepys both knew the story well
as children.

Enham Alamein became a home for modern heroes, acquiring
the second part of its name after the famous battle fought to pre-
vent Egypt falling to the Germans in the second world war. The
Egyptian government honoured this place with the extra name. It
became a home and centre for disabled servicemen.

## The Walk

**1.** Face the Institute and go left to pass the Enham Trust shop on
your right and come level with the thatched bus shelter on
the Green across the road on your left. Turn right, as sign-
posted for the Charity Shop car park. Continue up the lane to
where it terminates with a stile giving access to a field ahead.
Cross this stile and walk along the right-hand edge of the
field, turning left in the corner ahead to pass woodland on
your right.

**2.** Turn right over a stile to take a woodland path. Continue with
woodland on your left and fields on your right. Cross a stile
ahead and turn right along a track. Fork left to emerge at a
roadside. Go right to pass the Hare and Hounds pub and fork
left along a quiet lane (the course of the Roman road).

**3.** Go ahead at a T-junction to remain with the Roman road,
which is now a hedged track (NB not the farm track forking
right). Follow this across another road and at the next road,
bear right. Pass a road on your right, then reach a road on your

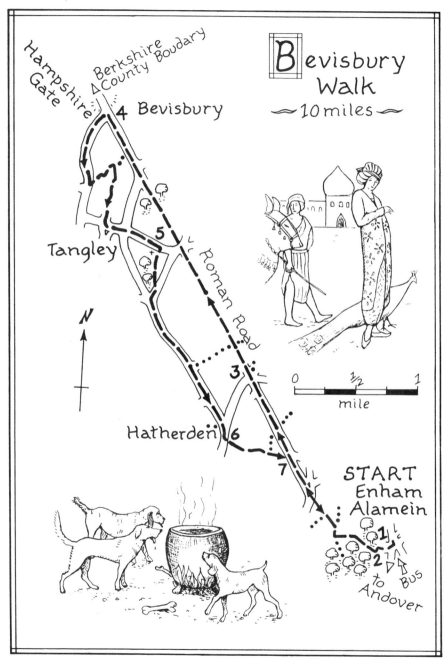

Bevisbury Walk
~10 miles~

Hampshire Gate

Berkshire County Boundary

△ 4 Bevisbury

Tangley

5

N ↑

Roman Road

3

0    ½    1
mile

Hatherden 6

7

START
Enham
Alamein

1
2

to Andover
BUS

left. At the corner ahead on your left can be seen the earthworks of Bevisbury (also on your right).

**4.** Take the road on your left sign-posted for Clanville and Weyhill. Turn sharply left up a sign-posted bridle way and reach a
junction with another track where you turn sharply right.
Pass the Cricketers Arms and emerge on a road. Go left and
soon bear left at a fork. Go ahead at a cross-roads with a war
memorial and telephone box.

**5.** Turn right at St Thomas of Canterbury's Church, Tangley,
passing it on your right to take a sign-posted footpath which
goes through some attractive woodland. Bear right at a road to
reach a junction, where you go left at the Fox Inn, as sign-
posted for Hatherden and Andover. Go through Hatherden,
passing Christ Church on your right. Look for a stile on your
left as you approach the Hamster pub.

**6.** Turn left over the stile to take a sign-posted path which runs
beside the hedge on your right. Go ahead over a stile in the
corner and through the next field to a stile near the left-hand
corner. Bear left into the next field and go right, keeping the
hedge on your right in the following field. Pass a hedged path
on your left to go ahead through another field and come to a
lane. This is the Roman road of your outward route.

**7.** Go right to retrace your steps to the bus stop in Enham
Alamein. Remember to fork left after the Hare and Hounds
pub. Look for a stile on your left after a track has come in
sharply from the left to join yours. Turn left over this stile to
take the woodland path back to Enham Alamein.

# 4. Abra Barrow

**Route:** Overton – Abra Barrow – Laverstoke – Overton

**Distance:** 8 miles. Moderate.

**Maps:** O.S. Pathfinders 1203 Kingsclere and 1223 Whitcburch, O.S. Landranger 185 Winchester & Basingstoke.

**Start:** Overton railway station (SU 517508).

**Access:** Trains run to Overton from London Waterloo, Basingstoke, Salisbury and Exeter. Buses (nos 75 & 76) run from Basingstoke and Salisbury.

## Abra Barrow

This long barrow is situated lower than expected, with good reason. Jon Appleton has shared his knowledge of the alignments converging on the tumulus near the eastern entrance of the hill fort on Danebury Hill (Walk 9) in The Ley Hunter no 109. Abra Barrow would seem to owe its location to the Beltane and Lughnasadh sunrise, as seen from Danebury on 5 May and 8 August. This line has an angle of 63 degrees and is marked by two tumuli north of Charity Down Farm plus an interesting mound on the ridge taken by the road between Longstock and Goodworth Clatford. When viewed from Danebury, Abra Barrow is on the horizon, some 13 miles to the north-east. This Beltane/Lughnasadh sunrise line is a most important one, as Paul Devereux's insights at Silbury Hill revealed (see Walks in Mysterious Wiltshire). Beltane marked the beginning of summer and prehistoric peoples probably held vigils to witness the life-giving sunrise, along with a bonfire to encourage the light, as well as other rites to do with the season of fertility. Lughnasadh was the time of harvest and a festival of thankful joy. Our ancestors so revered these important sunrises that they saw fit to build this barrow here.

## The Walk

**1.** Go right from the station and turn left to follow the pavement of the B3051 into Overton, passing St Mary's Church on your right. Turn right along the High Street, reach Southington and look for a track sign-posted as a footpath on your left at Butcher's Cottage (no 3 Southington). Go up this enclosed path.

**2.** Turn right along a hedged track and turn left at a junction to walk south for nearly two miles.

**3.** Turn right along a track sign-posted as a footpath, initially with trees on your left, then beside a hedge on your right. Go ahead over a stile and continue with a fence on your right. Turn right in the next corner and pass a tumulus in the field on your right. Reach a path junction on your left, waymarked by yellow arrows.

**4.** You will take the waymarked path now on your left, but first go ahead uphill with a hedge on your left and come to Abra Barrow, just to the right of the path. Retrace your steps to the junction and turn right to walk beside a hedge on your left in a westerly direction. The track has a hedge on both sides after the first field. Turn left to pass Pot Bottom Cottage on your right.

**5.** Turn right to pass Laverstock Grange farmhouse on your right (the stables are on your left). Turn right to go down the right-hand edge of the first field on your right after the house and gardens Descend with a hedge on your right, then climb and continue with the hedge on your right in the next field over

# Abra Barrow Walk
## ～8 miles～

Abra Barrow marks the Beltane (May 1st) sunrise from Danebury Hill (66°NE)

Horizon

Abra Barrow

Tumulus

Tumulus

Long Barrow

Danebury Hill

N

START 1 to London Waterloo

to Salisbury

Overton

2

N

Remains of St Mary's Church

LINK WITH WALK 6 AT ITS DIRECTION POINT 5

to Whitchurch

Laverstoke Park

B3400

6

Freefolk

3

Beltane Sunrise to Danebury Hillfort

Abra Barrow

4

0 ½ 1
mile

Laverstoke Grange Farm

5

the brow of the hill. Take the path ahead through woodland to descend to the B3400 road.

***If you wish to link this route with walk 6, go left to its direction point 5. Otherwise:***

6.  Turn right along the pavement of the road to Overton. Turn left down Southington Lane, cross the River Test and turn right along Silk Mill Lane. Keep right along Court Drove and Church Road to pass St Mary's Church on your left and turn left down Kingsclere Road to return to the railway station, on your right.

# 5. Deadman's Plack

***Route:***    Andover Down – Faulkner's Down Farm – Test Way –
Longparish – Patchington Copse – Deadman's Plack –
Andover Down.

***Distance:*** 9½ miles. Moderate.

***Maps:***     O.S. Pathfinders 1222 Andover and 1223 Whitchurch,
O.S. Landranger 185 Winchester & Basingstoke.

***Start:***    Bus stop at turn for Andover Down Farm (SU 403463).

***Access:***   Andover Down Farm bus stop is served by nos 60/61
(Winchester – Andover – Newbury) and 76 (Salisbury –
Andover – Basingstoke). Some buses run via
Longparish (direction point 4). Tel. 01256 464501 or
0345 023067 for times.

## A Sacrificial Murder?

Deadman's Plack Monument takes the form of a tall stone cross.
Dowsing for leys going through it brought a line running 66 degrees (deduct 4 from 70 to allow for magnetic variation) to the
north-east and not far off the Beltane (May Day) sunrise line. This
could link the monument with the old churches at Freefolk and
Laverstoke Park (see Walk 6). This information (and it is as relevant to the Lugnasadh sunrise in early August) may suggest a
deeper meaning to what purports to be a straightforward murder.

The monument was erected in 1835 by Colonel Iremonger, the
owner of Wherwell Priory (SU 390410). It commemorates the
murder of Aethelwald, Ealdorman of Hampshire, by King Aedgar
of Wessex so that the king could marry his widow Aelfrida,

daughter of Ordgar, Ealdorman of Devon. Aethelwald had origi-
nally been sent by the king to check if reports of Aelfrida's beauty
were true. Falling in love with her himself, he sent back the mes-
sage that she was too ugly to become the queen, whilst Aethei-
wald generously married her himself. When the king paid a visit
on the couple and discovered Aelfrida's true looks, he was angry
at the deception, while Aelfrida realised that she should have
been married to the king. Legend tells how the two connived at
Aethelwald's murder on this very spot in the woods. As a queen,
Aelfrida gained further notoriety with the death of her step-son
Edward the Martyr in Corfe Castle in 979, four years after King
Aedgar's death. This led to her own son, Aethelred (the Unready)
succeeding to the throne. This event belongs to a book of 'Walks
in Mysterious Dorset', but Margaret Murray postulates in The Divine King in England that Edward had to die so young because of
the appearance of a comet (presaging disaster), followed by a fam-
ine, then a floor giving way at a national council, killing many important people. God had to be appeased by the sacrifice of a royal
victim. William Rufus may have suffered a similar death will-
ingly (see Walk 21). She was obviously an accomplished witch
and may have sharpened her skills by practising blood sacrifice
at an appropriate site, on an important ley, on her unfortunate
first husband.

Perhaps stricken by remorse, after the martyrdom of Edward,
Aelfrida became a nun and founded the nunnery at Wherwell, on
the banks of the Test three miles south of Deadman's Plack.
Strange lights have been reported hovering over the burial place
of Wherwell's nuns. The priory at Wherwell is also where a duck
is said to have laid an egg in the crypt. Hatched by a toad, it produced a cockatrice (a dragon-like creature). This grew to menace
the local inhabitants, until a man named Green attracted it with a
shiny mirror and killed it with a long spear in a part of Harewood
Forest still known as Green's Copse. The locals are said not to eat
duck's eggs now.

## The Walk

**1.** Cross the road from the bus stop to take the access lane to Andover Down Farm. Pass a timber yard and continue through a gate along a track which keeps to the edge of a field on your left and bears right past a house and woodland on your right. Continue beside a hedge on your right to reach Faulkner's Down Farm.

**2.** Turn right to pass the farm on your left. Turn right along a track waymarked as the Test Way, walking with a hedge on your right and going through a waymarked gap ahead. Turn left around the left-hand edge of the next field. Cross a stile and go left to a road. Cross the road to continue with the Test Way, soon passing woodland on your right, then taking a lane through the wood.

**3.** When level with gates giving access to a road on your right, go left with the track. Turn right at a sign-posted junction and walk with a hedge on your right. Follow Sugar Lane into Longparish.

**4.** Turn right past bus stops and the Plough Inn. When the road bends to the right, go straight ahead. Take a kissing-gate to pass St Nicholas' Church on your right, go through another kissing-gate and through two more fields. Maintain your direction along a lane, but when it bends right, go straight ahead with a track waymarked as the Test Way.

**5.** Bear right with the sign-posted Test Way along a narrow, enclosed, path. Go ahead across the A303 with care and follow the track waymarked as the Test Way. Turn right at a junction and climb to a road.

**6.** Go left some 50 metres then turn right with the sign-posted Test Way. Pass the course of a dismantled railway and bear left with the waymarked Test Way. Follow a concrete lane past buildings of a pig farm, bear right and turn left to leave

Patchingdon Piggery behind you and take the concrete lane through woodland. Bear right with the lane to pass a row of three more long pig sheds in Patchington Copse.

7. About 100 metres after the last pig shed, step over a chain stretched across the track and reach a crosstracks with a footpath sign on your right. Leave the Test Way by turning right. Bear left at a fork to climb through woodland to a crossing where there are gates on your left. Turn right to walk east through the forest, ignoring an initial track on your left and reaching a junction of several tracks.

8. Turn left to head north along a concrete lane. This bears right to the A303. Cross this road carefully and go left along its verge, very soon ignoring a sign-posted stile on your right. Do turn right with a track heading for the woods. Fork left and come to another fork where the right of way bears left. Fork right to approach the monument of Deadman's Plack. A narrow path on your right leads to it. Resume your previous track and direction and go right at a junction. Continue across a forest track, down through pasture and join a road.

9. Turn right along the road and come to a stile on your left. Turn left over this to follow the sign-posted path through a field and past trees on your left. Go ahead through woodland (Green's Copse is on your right), continue across a track and follow the path to emerge at the B3400 beside the bus stop.

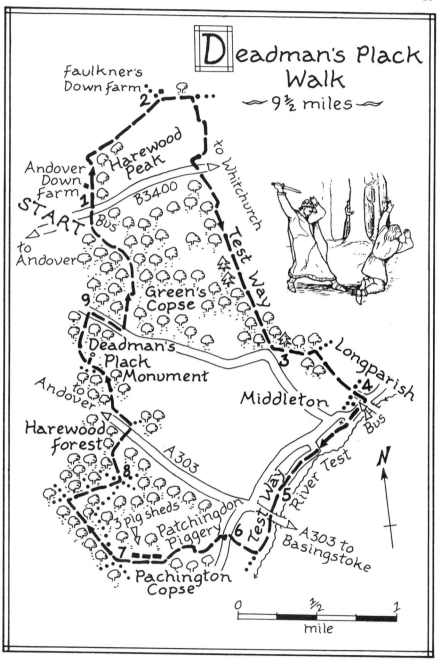

Deadman's Plack Walk ～9½ miles～

Faulkner's Down Farm

2

Harewood Peak

to Whitchurch

Andover Down Farm

1

B3400

START

Bus

to Andover

Test Way

Green's Copse

9

Deadman's Plack Monument

to Andover

3

Longparish

Middleton

4

Bus

Harewood Forest

A303

8

River Test

N

3 pig sheds

Patchingdon Piggery

Test Way

5

A303 to Basingstoke

7

6

Pachington Copse

0    ½    1
mile

# 6. Freefolk

**Route:**   Whitchurch – Harroway – Freefolk – Whitchurch

**Distance:** 6 miles. Easy.

**Maps:**    O.S. Pathfinder 1223 Whitchurch, O.S. Landranger 185 Winchester & Basingstoke.

**Start:**   Whitchurch railway station (SU 463489).

**Access:**  Trains run to Whitchurch from London Waterloo, Basingstoke, Salisbury and Exeter. Bus no 60 links Whitchurch with Winchester and Newbury, while nos 75 and 76 come from Salisbury and Basingstoke.

## Freya's Folk

Alfred Watkins listed a ley from Harewood Peak to Deane Church via the Victorian church dedicated to St Mary at Freefolk and the ruins of the old church in Laverstock Park, also dedicated to St Mary, in his book The Ley Hunter's Manual. This is interesting, as is the reference to the prehistoric Harroway in Watkins' seminal book The Old Straight Track. Watkins revealed that he adopted the word ley for these sighted tracks after reading Dr Williams-Freeman's description of following the Harroway in this area, including Finkley, near Andover. Watkins maintained that the ley appendage to Fink meant more than just a clearing in woodland and was much older than the Saxons. The true meaning of the word comes in the phrase 'the lay of the land', while its straight nature is reflected in the term 'lay' for aiming a gun.

Watkins didn't comment on the ley I dowsed at the old church in Freefolk, however. This suggested a link with the Beltane/Lug-

The tomb of Sir Richard Powlett, St Mary's church

nasadh sunrise and seemed to pass the ruined church dedicated to St Mary in Laverstoke Park. Turning to my map, I discovered that Deadman's Plack was also on this line (see Walk 5). Then I read in the church guide that Freefolk's church could have been built on the site of a pagan place of worship to the Goddess Frig. Frig, or Freya, would have been the Saxon version of the goddess of love and fertility. My personal feelings were that this was a spot where the Celts had honoured Rhiannon. Freefolk obviously refers to Frig's people. The church was mentioned in the Domesday Book and contains the tomb of Sir Richard Powlett, with his effigy, dated 1614. There is some evidence for a medieval wall painting of St Christopher, so ramblers will be blessed when entering this redundant church.

One night in a dream on the sacred peak of Cam Ingli in Wales, the goddess (Rhiannon) appeared as a very tall, noble figure.

Around her, linking hands, were tiny figures of men dancing in a circle by the light of the full moon. If this is a spot granting men the privilege of meeting the goddess and knowing her love, perhaps the free people would have chosen to so honour her here.

## The Walk

1. Go right from the station and pass Greenwoods (a No Through Road) on your right, then the Railway Inn on your left. Turn right and soon bear right off the road to take the sign-posted footpath past backs of houses on your right. Reach the course of a dismantled railway and turn right to pass under the surviving railway and go ahead until a stile beside double gates on your left. Cross the stile and turn right to walk beside a hedge on your right.

2. Turn right over a bridge across the old railway and go ahead along the right-hand edge of a field to a road. Turn left along its verge, then go right with a lane sign-posted for Woolding (this is the Harroway). Pass the first lane on your right.

3. Turn right along the second lane, Watch Lane, towards Freefolk. After crossing a bridge over the railway (the line between Salisbury and Basingstoke), take the first turning on your left, as sign-posted for the Walled Garden, Laverstoke Park.

4. Turn right along a sign-posted footpath through a field and down a narrow path past the Victorian church dedicated to St Mary, on your right. Descend to the main road.

*If you wish to link this route with walk 4, go left to its direction point 6.*

5. Go right 20 metres and turn left along a lane sign-posted for St Nicholas' Church. Pass this redundant church on your left and follow the track uphill. Pass a house on your right and

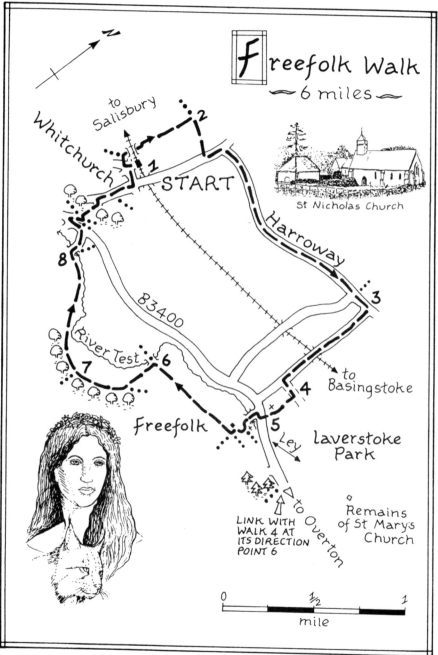

**F reefolk Walk**
~ 6 miles ~

to Salisbury

Whitchurch

2

1

START

St Nicholas Church

Harroway

8

B3400

River Test

3

7

6

to Basingstoke

4

Freefolk

5 Ley

laverstoke Park

LINK WITH WALK 4 AT ITS DIRECTION POINT 6

to Overton

Remains of St Mary's Church

0       ½       1
mile

soon turn right to take a path between fields and emerge past a house on your right at a lane near a bridge.

6.  Go left before the bridge and fork left with a waymarked path. Bear left through a field and turn right to walk along the foot of a wooded slope on your left.

7.  Don't take the waymarked path going over a stile on your left! Fork right along the floor of a valley, crossing a stile and walking past trees. Emerge over a stile and go ahead along the right-hand edges of three fields.

8.  Turn right across a footbridge and fork left along a lane. Go left at a road. Turn sharply right at Lynch Hill, then go left at a junction with a higher path and walk with trees on your right Soon turn right up a sunken path. Go left at its top, along King's Walk, then turn right along the pavement of Newbury Road. Turn left at Station Road to come back to the railway station, on your right.

# 7. Aldershot

**Route:** Aldershot railway station – Ash Lock – Basingstoke Canal – Pondtail – Fleet railway station

**Distance:** 7½ miles. Easy.

**Maps:** O.S. Pathfinder 1205 Farnborough & Aldershot, O.S. Landranger 186 Aldershot & Guildford.

**Start:** Aldershot railway station (SU 866504).

**Finish:** Fleet railway station (SU 816552).

**Access:** Trains run to Aldershot from London Waterloo and Alton, while another line links Aldershot with Ascot and Guildford. Fleet is on the line between Basingstoke and London Waterloo. If you want to travel by train between Fleet and Aldershot, change at Brookwood. A convenient link between the two ends of this linear walk are buses nos 10 and 12 running from Reading to Aldershot via Fleet (tel. 01252 315900 for times).

**Little Green Men**

This is a serious book, taking the walker to sites of ancient legends and mysterious deeds. You may think the ley lines are a product of my imagination, but I certainly don't. You can dowse them for yourself, while there's no arguing with the existence of strange ancient monuments. The latter half of the 20th century has generated its own folklore, linked to the perception that we are not alone in the universe. Space flight has expanded our horizons. We may not see fairies any longer (actually some claim to do, but don't want to attract even more disbelief and ridicule), but we do see little green men emerging from UFOs. Some would say they stem from the same source within our own minds. Others affirm that there are other worlds and dimensions to this world which we can sometimes glimpse. There may even be nuts and bolts space craft landing here with little humanoids wearing green space suits and helmets. I have no direct personal knowledge of them and would prefer to avoid possible entanglements with frauds. I only investigated this case because it happened in an area of Hampshire which might otherwise have been overlooked. The Aldershot area is rich in army camps, people, buildings, roads and railways – all the things the rambler normally tries to escape from. Military installations occupy possibly interesting places, such as Puckridge Hill (across the canal at the midway point on this walk). Then I read 'UFOs Over Hampshire and the Isle of Wight' by Robert Price and realised that there was a mystery linked to the Basingstoke Canal at Aldershot. The towpath of the Basingstoke Canal is an excellent route for a walk, following an attractive wildlife corridor. Opened in 1794 as a means of bringing agricultural produce to London, this canal served the building of the barracks at Aldershot in 1854 before succumbing to competition from the railways. It proved useful for transporting munitions in World War II and has now been restored for leisure use.

So, there was good reason to walk here. The story featured Alfred Burtoo, a 78 year-old angler who was casting his rod from a spot on the canal bank between Ash Lock and the railway bridge at Aldershot around 1 am on August 12, 1983. He saw a bright light in the sky, approaching from the south. After flying low over the railway, this UFO landed behind trees near the canal towpath. Little green men did indeed appear and led the curious Alfred into their flying saucer. Asked his age, the intrepid angler was told he was too old for the aliens' purposes. Having returned to his fishing, he witnessed the spacecraft take off and head westwards.

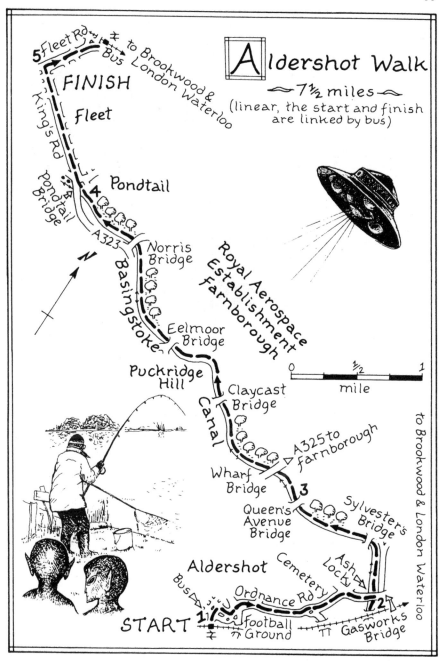

Aldershot Walk
~7½ miles~
(linear, the start and finish
are linked by bus)

FINISH
Fleet
Fleet Rd
5
Bus
to Brookwood &
London Waterloo
King's Rd
Pondtail
Bridge
4
Pondtail
A323
Norris
Bridge
Basingstoke
Royal Aerospace
Establishment
Farnborough
Eelmoor
Bridge
Puckridge
Hill
Claycast
Bridge
Canal
A325 to
Farnborough
Wharf
Bridge
3
Queen's
Avenue
Bridge
Sylvester's
Bridge
Aldershot
Cemetery
Ash
Lock
to Brookwood & London Waterloo
Bus
Ordnance Rd
2
START
1
Football
Ground
Gasworks
Bridge

0      ½      1
mile

N

André Grandjean

Such a story is only worth repeating if the witness can be considered honest and reliable. Alfred Burtoo attained the age of 80 before dying in 1986, so it was impossible to interview him. However, I did discuss the incident with André Grandjean, the Match Secretary of the Basingstoke Canal Anglers' Association, for whom Alfred Burtoo had served as a bailiff. Fishermen are notorious for telling tales, but I found Mr Grandjean a level-headed man who had known Alfred Burtoo, respected his integrity and felt he had to accept that he told the truth. The proximity of military establishments may be relevant, but would you expect the Ministry of Defence to tell us if aliens had landed?

## The Walk

*1.* With your back to Aldershot railway station and with the bus station ahead on your left, bear right along Arthur Street. Turn right in the direction of the football ground, with its prominent floodlight pylons, but turn left at a cross-roads to follow Windsor Way to a roundabout. Go ahead along Ordnance Road and continue past a cemetery on your left after a roundabout. Pass Gallwey Road on your left and turn right along Government Road. Cross a bridge over the Basingstoke Canal.

2. Turn right along the towpath of the Basingstoke Canal to walk past trees on your left, with the canal on your right. Reach the bridge carrying the railway over the canal that features in Alfred Burtoo's account of the UFO. Turn around to retrace your steps, with the canal now on your left. Go under the road bridge and pass Ash Lock. Continue past Sylvester's Bridge and under Queen's Avenue Bridge.

3. Go ahead, keeping the canal on your left and pass under the bridge carrying the A325. After three more bridges, approach Pondtail Bridge, where there are houses on your right.

4. Leave the canal towpath just before it goes under Pondtail Bridge. Bear right to emerge with Pondtail Road going right. Cross it to take King's Road ahead, ignoring Aldershot Road, which forks left.

5. Turn right at the T-junction to follow Fleet Road to Fleet railway station, on your right. Buses nos 10 and 12 run from here back to Aldershot railway station.

# 8. Abbotts Ann

**Route:**  Abbotts Ann – Abbotts Ann Down – Dunkirt Barn –
Abbotts Ann

**Distance:** 4 miles. Easy.

**Maps:**  O.S. Pathfinder 1222 Andover, O.S. Landranger 185
Winchester & Basingstoke.

**Start:**  The Eagle pub, Abbotts Ann (SU 329435).

**Access:**  Bus no 76 runs to Abbotts Ann from Andover,
Basingstoke and Salisbury.

## Virgins' Crowns

The church at Abbotts Ann isn't an old building. It was rebuilt in
1716 by Thomas Pitt, a forebear of William Pitt, Prime Minister
and Earl of Chatham, who financed the work out of a fortune he
had made in India (he sold an enormous diamond to the Regent of
France). The church it replaced dated back to at least Saxon
times, perhaps even the earliest days of Christianity in Roman
Britain. There was a villa near Dunkirt Farm which had central
heating in the fourth century. By the end of the fifth century Cerdic had landed to conquer his kingdom in Hampshire and to lay
the foundations of Wessex. This enigmatic character, probably of
mixed Celtic and Saxon or Jutish descent, is dealt with elsewhere
(see Walk 17). No doubt, this was an even older sacred site. Ann
was the reputedly British grandmother of Jesus. Perhaps there is a
very ancient special reason for this particular place recognising
virginity with so much honour. In the Middle Ages it was deemed
worthy to die a virgin and those who qualified were awarded vir-

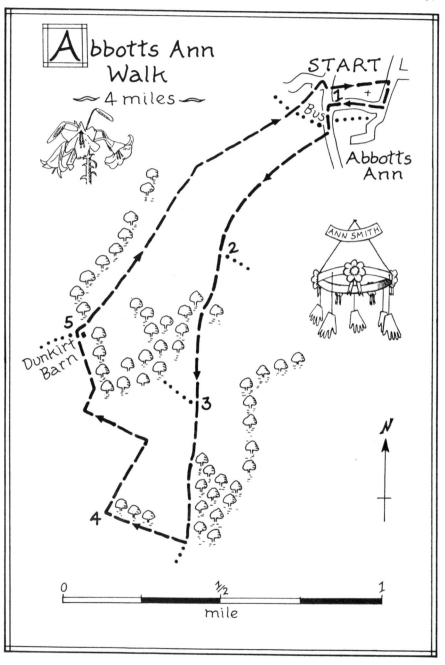

Abbotts Ann
Walk
~ 4 miles ~

START / L

Bus

Abbotts
Ann

ANN SMITH

2

5
Dunkirt
Barn

3

4

N

0          ½          1
        mile

gins' crowns. This practice survives in Abbots Ann. A crown is awarded to any unmarried person of good character, whether man or woman, who has been born, baptised and who dies within the parish. These crowns are made of hazelwood and decorated with white paper rosettes. Challengers who dispute an award are confronted by five paper gauntlets attached to each crown. Attached to a wand, the crown is carried by two girls dressed in white at the funeral procession, before being hung from the gallery of the church for three weeks so that all who enter must pass beneath it. Provided there is no successful challenge in that period, the crown is then hung on the wall of the church with a plate bearing the deceased's name and dates. Myra Annetts died in 1973 aged 73. The earliest surviving crown dates from John Morrant in 1740.

Nearby Weyhill (to the north of Abbotts Ann and west of Andover) was where a man sold his wife at a fair held at this ancient cross-roads and inspired a similar incident in Thomas Hardy's novel 'The Mayor of Casterbridge'.

### The Walk

1.  Face the Eagle pub and go right, soon passing the post office on your right. Fork right up a lane sign-posted as a public footpath (ignoring a narrow footpath sign-posted going sharp right). The surface of the lane soon deteriorates to 'green' status.

2.  Don't bear left between fields with a farm track! Go straight ahead along the hedged green lane. Emerge to bear left with a sign-posted path through a field.

3.  Go ahead along a hedged track between fields, then past woodland on your left. Take a gap into the corner of the field ahead and immediately turn right to walk beside a hedge on your right.

4.  Follow the path around a corner on your right and take a

sign-posted path ahead, passing woodland on your right at first, then walking beside a hedge on your right. Turn left in a corner to head for Dunkirt Barn.

5. Turn right along a track which leads back to Abbotts Ann. Go right at a road junction, then, just before the Eagle pub, turn left along a path to St Mary's Church. Continue past the church on your right. Turn right at a road and turn right again at its end to come back to the Eagle pub, on your right.

# 9. Danebury Hill

*Route:*      Stockbridge – Meon Hill – Shepherd's Bush –
              Danebury Hill – Longstock – Stockbridge

*Distance:* 8 miles. Moderate.

*Maps:*       O.S. Pathfinder 1242 The Wallops, O.S. Landranger
              185 Winchester & Basingstoke.

*Start:*      St Peter's Church, Stockbridge (SU 356351).

*Access:*   Bus no 68 links Stockbridge with Winchester and
            Salisbury, while no 99 comes from Andover.

**Danebury Ring**

The impressive hillfort at Danebury has been excavated by Pro-
fessor Barry Cunliffe and featured on television programmes. It
has revealed much about life in the Iron Age, as can be seen in the
museum at Andover, There is much more to discover about the
significance of this site, surrounded by chalk downland. The
Ordnance Survey erected their trig point on a tumulus outside
the eastern gateway of the hillfort. This tumulus dates from the
Neolithic period, making it more than twice as old as the Iron Age
camp. Intriguingly, it also seems to be the focus of several leys or
spirit paths, including the line followed by the path on this route
between Meon Hill and Shepherd's Bush. These alignments
formed the subject of an article by Jon Appleton in The Ley
Hunter no 109. He came here to investigate post holes big enough
to take tree trunks a metre in width found near the tumulus.
Aware that these could have been early astronomical markers,
Appleton discovered that the two long barrows to the north-west

Danebury Hillfort

of Danebury were on the midsummer sunset and maximum north moon set lines. The long barrow to the north-east was on the sunrise line around the time of Beltane and Lughnassadh (see Walk 4 – Abra Barrow). Also in the north-east, the summer solstice sunrise line has the village of Hannington on the horizon. Here the churchyard's raised enclosure is at the end of a line which the Landranger map shows passing through a long barrow at 507526, near Willesley Farm. The line for the most northerly moonrise meets the horizon on Watership Down, with an intermediate tumulus at Angledown. Farley Mount (see Walk 11) marks the most southerly moonrise position. A tumulus on the horizon in Crab Wood is on the winter solstice sunrise line, while sunrise at Imbolc and Samhain (at the beginning of February and November) passes The Beacon on its way to a long barrow on Salt Hill, south of East Meon. The most southerly moonset appears over a mound on Whiteshoot Hill known as The Turret. Another mound marks the line of the midwinter sunset. A tumulus on the northern slopes of Suddern Hill indicates the equinox line. A pair of aligned tumuli just south of Beacon Hill indicate the Beltane and Lughnassadh sunset line, while the summer solstice sunset is over the terraced slopes of Quarley Hill, actually reaching the horizon at 246443 where a mound stood beside a dew pond at the end of an ancient earthwork.

Just to the west of Danebury are the Wallops (Over Wallop, Middle Wallop and Nether Wallop). Wallop was where a battle was fought in AD 473 between Ambrosius and Vitalinus, a relative of the tyrant Vortigern. Ambrosius won and may have done so in such a manner that he gave the word 'wallop' to our vocabulary. Also known as the Battle of Guoloph, wallop or wiell-hop probably refers to an empty or dry river.

## The Walk

1. Face St Peter's Church in Stockbridge and go left. Cross a bridge over the River Test. Climb with the road ahead but when it bends right, keep straight ahead along Roman Road, which soon becomes a hedged track over Meon Hill.

2. Bear right across a stile to take the sign-posted path, walking beside a hedge on your right. Cross a road, continue over the stile ahead and along the right-hand of a field. Pass a stile on your right. Go ahead with the ley towards the tumulus and trig. point on the eastern side of Danebury Hill. Bear left with the headland path at Shepherd's Bush (a white thorn tree).

3. Turn right along a hedged track. Go left at a road and bear left along the access road to Danebury Hillfort. Explore the earthworks, now shaded by beech trees.

4. Retrace your steps to the road and go right. Pass a road on your left and the track used to reach here on your right. Fork left along a track to pass a wedge of trees on your right.

5. Reach St Mary's Church, Longstock. Turn left along a road,

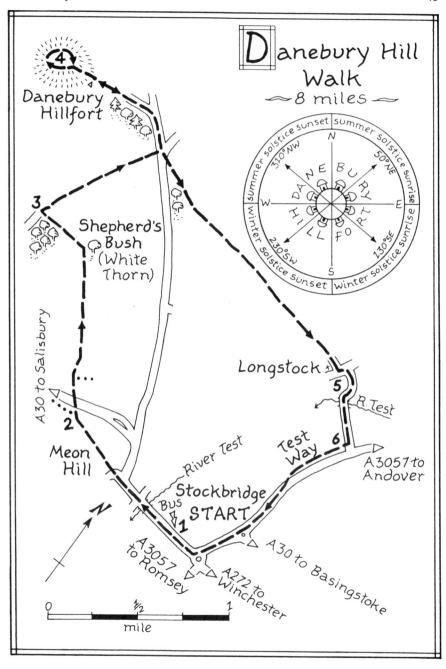

Danebury Hill
Walk
~8 miles~

Danebury Hillfort

Shepherd's
Bush
(White
Thorn)

3

A30 to Salisbury

2

Meon
Hill

Longstock

5

R. Test

Test Way

6

A3057 to Andover

River Test

Stockbridge
START

1

Bus

A3057 to Romsey

A272 to Winchester

A30 to Basingstoke

0    ½    1
mile

summer solstice sunset | summer solstice sunrise
310°NW        N        50°NE
W                              E
230°SW        S        130°SE
winter solstice sunset | winter solstice sunrise

DANEBURY HILL FORT

then turn right down The Bunny to follow this road across the River Test.

6.  Turn right with the sign-posted Test Way. This follows the course of a dismantled railway before merging with the road on your left. Pass one roundabout, reach a second round-about and go right back into Stockbridge.

# 10. Tidbury Ring

**Route:**   South  Wonston – Wonston  Manor  Farm – Sutton Scotney – possible extension to Tidbury Ring – Sutton Scotney – West Stoke Farm – South Wonston

**Distance:** 7 or 11½ miles. Easy.

**Maps:**   O.S. Pathfinders 1223 Whitchurch and 1243 Winchester North, O.S. Landranger 185 Winchester & Basingstoke.

**Start:**   Bus stop in West Hill Road North, South Wonston (SU 472359).

**Access:**  Buses nos 60 and 61 run to South Wonston from Winchester, Andover and Newbury.

## The Winchester Ley

This walk may be extended to visit Tidbury Ring (NB. along a private farm track) if you wish to dowse the ley which links this prehistoric earthwork with Winchester Cathedral and St Catherine's Hill (Walk 12). At a compass bearing of 352 degrees (356 less 4 degrees for magnetic variation) when facing north (172 degrees when facing south, as recorded by Paul Devereux and Ian Thomson in The Ley Hunter's Companion), the ley can also be examined at the long barrow near the start of this walk in South Wonston. Unfortunately, this long barrow barely manages a rise now, but at least it has been preserved in an open space between new houses. If you find it hard to believe it is really there, do ask the locals, who remember it as an impressive 100 metres in length. Another long barrow used to exist nearby.

Tidbury Ring is in much healthier shape. The remains of Roman buildings have been uncovered within the ring, where coins have also been found. You can look southwards down the ley from just to the east of the ring's southern entrance, towards Winchester, whose cathedral stands on an ancient sacred site.

## The Walk

1. Alight at the bus stop on West Hill Road North, South Wonston. All buses travel around South Wonston in the same clockwise direction, so there is a bus stop on only one side of the road. Go north, soon passing Waverley Drive on your right, then Wrights Way on your left. Pass an unnamed track between houses on your right. The open space next on your right, before Goldfinch Way, is the site of the long barrow on the ley between Tidbury Ring and Winchester Cathedral. Go ahead past Goldfinch Way on your right. Go ahead to a road junction and turn left along a sign-posted right of way. Follow this old hedged track to South Wonston Farm.

2. Turn right along a sign-posted bridleway. This track cuts across the course of a dismantled railway to reach Wonston Manor Farm. Go left, as waymarked by blue arrows, then right to pass the farm buildings. Ignore a lane on your left as you take the farm access lane ahead to a sign-posted junction with bridleways.

3. Go left with the metalled lane to reach a road. Go right along the road for 20 metres, then turn left to take a sign-posted public footpath. This bears right in the far corner to head for the village of Sutton Scotney.

4. Go left to a road junction, where you turn right and pass the Coach & Horses pub on your left. Bear right to a roundabout.

5. If you are not taking the extension of this walk to Tidbury Ring, continue with direction POINT 6. If you are proceeding by road and private track to Tidbury Ring, to dowse the ley, go left along the pavement of the A30 (Bullington Lane), reach a

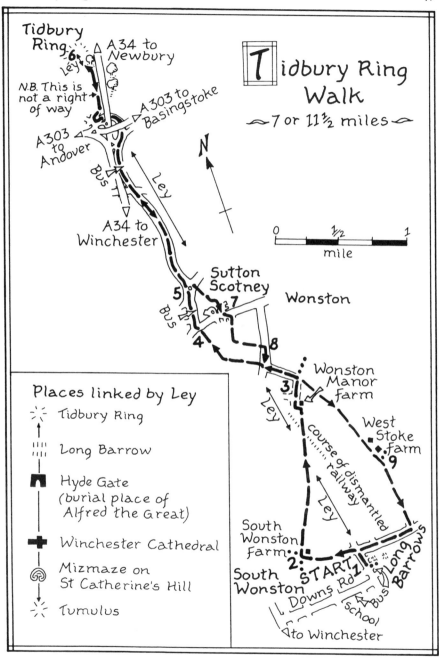

Tidbury Ring

A34 to Newbury

N.B. This is not a right of way

A303 to Basingstoke

A303 to Andover

Ley

Bus

A34 to Winchester

Ley

N

# Tidbury Ring Walk

~7 or 11½ miles~

0    ½    1
mile

Sutton Scotney

5

7

Bus

4

8

Wonston

Wonston Manor Farm

3

Ley

course of dismantled railway

West Stoke Farm

9

## Places linked by Ley

Tidbury Ring

Long Barrow

Hyde Gate
(burial place of Alfred the Great)

Winchester Cathedral

Mizmaze on St Catherine's Hill

Tumulus

South Wonston Farm

Ley

2

South Wonston

START

Downs Rd

Long Barrows

Bus

school

to Winchester

major road junction and take the road bearing right which goes under a bridge supporting the A34. Turn right at the access lane for Tidbury Farm and immediately turn right again to climb with a private farm track which bears left to run parallel to the A34 on your right and gradually diverge from this road to head for Tidbury Ring, whose earthworks are clothed by trees, but with a gap for the southern entrance. Access to Tidbury Ring along this private farm track is only with the permission of the landowner and at your own risk. ***This is not a right of way.***

*6.* If you extended this route to Tidbury Ring, retrace your steps to direction point 5. All walkers take the sign-posted public footpath going through a kissing-gate beside a field-gate which is across the road from the garage near the roundabout. If you did not go to Tidbury Ring, you will find this path on your right. Pass a playing field and take an enclosed path in the far left corner to emerge along an access road for a small estate and reach its junction with a road. Go left along the pavement, soon passing Moorcroft Close on your right.

*7.* Turn right along a lane sign-posted as a public footpath. When this lane bends left, go straight ahead along a path way-marked by a yellow arrow. This hedged path turns left to take you to a road.

*8.* Go right to retrace part of your outward journey by taking the access lane to Wonston Manor Farm, on your left. This time, however, take the sign-posted bridleway ahead when the lane turns right to the farm. Follow this track past the buildings of West Stoke Farm, on your left.

*9.* Continue along the track to reach a road. Go right and come to the junction near the start of this walk. Turn left to retrace your steps past the long barrow, on your left, to the bus stop in West Hill Road North.

# 11. Farley Mount

**Route:**   King's Somborne – Clarendon Way – Farley Mount – Parnholt Wood – King's Somborne

**Distance:** 8 miles. Moderate.

**Maps:**    O.S. Pathfinders 1242 The Wallops, 1263 Romsey and 1264 Winchester (South), O.S. Landranger 185 Winchester & Basingstoke.

**Start:**   War Memorial bus stop, King's Somborne (SU 361310).

**Access:**  Bus no 68 runs to King's Somborne from Winchester and Salisbury, while no 99 comes from Andover.

## A Memorial to a Horse

Farley Mount today is known for its memorial to a horse. This takes the form of a 30 ft high pyramid, in the base of which is a shelter and a plaque on the wall telling about the horse. Sir Paulet John was riding the hunter in 1733 when it jumped into a 25 ft deep chalk pit, yet managed to avoid injury either to horse or rider. The lucky pair went on to win the Hunters' Cup at Winchester Races the next year, with the horse now called Beware Chalk Pit. Sir Paulet chose to bury the horse under this monument when it died in 1740. Was he aware of the significance of this spot? So often, it seems, people in the 18th century knew to build their memorials or follies on leys. Whether this was by conscious design or natural attraction is hard to say. As Jon Appleton outlined in The Ley Hunter no 109, the memorial at Farley Mount, which is built on top of a Bronze Age burial mound, marks the most southerly moonrise position as seen from the ancient tumulus near the eastern entrance to the hillfort at Danebury (see Walk 9).

The Roman road followed for a while on the outward section of this route was the link between Winchester and Old Sarum. Beacon Hill is one of a chain of such hills which have been the sites of hilltop beacons since prehistory to Napoleon.

## The Walk

1. Take Church Road, passing SS Peter & Paul's Church on your right. Ignore a sign-posted path on your right. Turn left along a road sign-posted for Winchester and Little Somborne.

2. Turn right with the sign-posted Clarendon Way, taking the left-hand edges of three fields. Go ahead over a stile and continue with the headland path to reach a stile in the far left corner. Bear left over this to follow a woodland path to a signpost.

3. Turn left along an old Roman road. Go straight ahead at a sign-posted track junction and continue with the Clarendon Way to a road.

4. As you approach the road, turn sharply right with the sign-posted Clarendon Way. Follow a fenced path around woodland on your right. Converge at a signpost with a track coming sharply from your right and go ahead to take a path on your right to visit the memorial to the horse.

5. Retrace your steps from the monument to the track and go left to return to the signpost. This time fork left. Ignore a sign-posted bridleway into Parnholt Wood on your right.

6. Reach a crosstracks and turn right to follow the main track through the wood, then as a fenced track through fields to a road.

7. Go left to a junction, where you go right to return to the start.

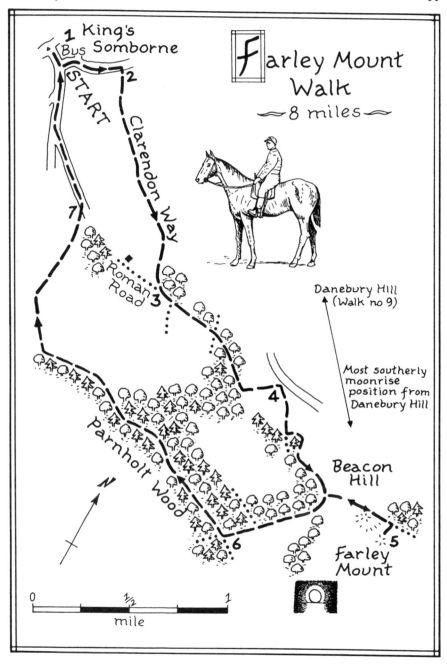

# Farley Mount Walk
## ~8 miles~

1 King's Somborne
Bus
START
2
Clarendon Way
7
Roman Road 3
Parnholt Wood
4
N
Beacon Hill
5
6
Farley Mount

Danebury Hill
(Walk no 9)

Most southerly
moonrise
position from
Danebury Hill

0 ½ 1
mile

# 12. Winchester

**Route:**     Winchester – St Catherine's Hill – St Cross –
              Winchester

**Distance:** 6½ miles. Strenuous.

**Maps:**      O.S. Pathfinder 1264 Winchester South. O.S.
              Landranger 165 Winchester & Basingstoke.

**Start:**     Winchester railway station (SU 478300).

**Access:**    Trains and buses run to Winchester from many places,
              including fast trains from London Waterloo and
              Weymouth, also express trains between Manchester
              and Poole via Birmingham and Oxford.

## King Alfred's Capital

Known to the Romans as Venta Belgarum, Winchester's history
extends well back into the mists of time. It was a place of great
temporal and spiritual power, with the area now containing the
cathedral believed to have been occupied by an ancient stone circle and, later, a Roman temple. 'Druid stones' and Roman temple
pillars are said to be incorporated into the present Norman building which, at 169 metres, is the second-longest medieval building
in the world. It replaced earlier Saxon cathedrals and was built on
a foundation of logs laid down in bogland. A drier spot would not
do, obviously. Guy Underwood dowsed the cathedral and found
special features, described in his The Pattern of the Past. Walk 10
in this book investigates the ley which comes from Tidbury Ring
to the cathedral and extends to the maze of St Catherine's Hill.
This ley went through the initial burial place of King Alfred the

The maze on St Catherine's Hill

Great in the old Hyde Abbey. Eight other Saxon kings are buried
here, as are Canute, William Rufus and the novelist Jane Austen.
The Christian saint with the powers of the Welsh druid that he
also was, Swithun, had his body transferred indoors on July 15,
971, after lying outside at his request since his death in 862. The
saint showed his disapproval by causing it to rain that day and for
the next 40 days. Capital of England from 829 to 1278, Winchester staged William the Conqueror's coronation. He was crowned
in London as well. The Domesday Book was compiled here,
while the first English Parliaments met in the Great Hall of the
castle. This has housed King Arthur's Round Table since it was
made in the 13th century, during the reign of King Henry III, who
was born here. Henry VII had his first son baptised Arthur here in
1486, while Henry VIII was responsible for the Round Table being painted and his likeness features as King Arthur. Geoffrey of
Monmouth placed Arthur's final struggle with Modred here,

which is nonsense, of course, but emphasises the importance and depth of history associated with Winchester.

How refreshing it is to find such a great city so intimately approachable. Wayfarers can even claim bread and beer from the porter's lodge at the Hospital of St Cross, founded in 1133 and the oldest charitable institution in Britain still doing its original work. The whole can be surveyed from the nature reserve of St Catherine's Hill. The medieval chapel erected within the Iron Age hillfort and now a ruin in an 18th century plantation of beech trees has an interesting dedication. UFOs could be compared to Catherine Wheels and several UFOs have been sighted around here. Nearby is a unique maze, because it is square (29 metres x 29 metres). This shape plus the fact that the path to be trodden by the pilgrim is denoted by the grooves between the turf ridges may suggest that the original design was lost in recent re-cutting. Such re-cutting was considered a punishment for pupils from Winchester College, including one unfortunate soul who had to remain at school during the holidays and cut 'Dolce Donum' (Home is sweet) on a tree before drowning himself in the River Itchen.

There is an uglier aspect to Winchester provided by the constant roar of traffic from the surrounding roads. The desecration of Twyford Down brought direct action from anti-roads protesters and it is easy to see and hear why. Magical, mysterious places such as this do not just belong to the past. They are in the present and should be safeguarded for future generations. How appropriate that this is where so many young Greens were moved to show their opposition to the planners, politicians, bureaucrats and road-builders who blight this country.

## The Walk

**1.** Walk into the city from the railway station, turning right along Sussex Street to reach Castle Hall and to see the Round Table. Facing the Castle Hall, go left down the High Street,

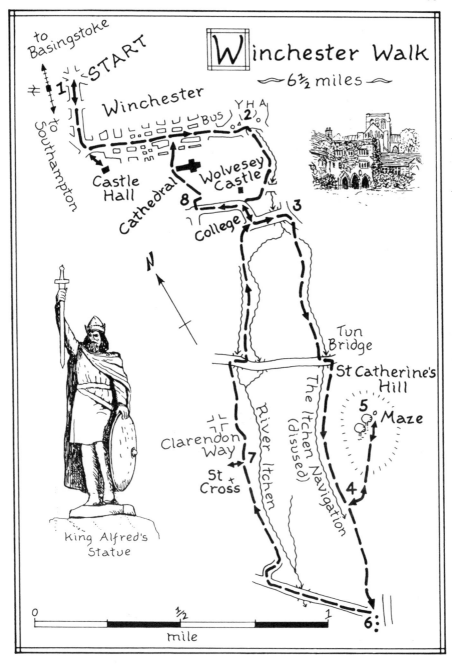

to Basingstoke

START

1

to Southampton

# Winchester Walk
~6½ miles~

Winchester

BUS

YHA 2

Castle Hall

Cathedral

Wolvesey Castle

8

College

3

N

Tun Bridge

St Catherine's Hill

5 Maze

Clarendon Way

River Itchen

The Itchen Navigation (disused)

7

St Cross

4

King Alfred's Statue

6

0    ½    1
mile

continue along the Broadway and reach King Alfred's statue.
Go ahead to where the City Mill and the youth hostel are on
your left.

2. Turn right along the sign-posted Riverside Walk, walking
downstream with the River Itchen on your left. Part of the
third century Roman city wall can be seen on your right. Continue with the city walls on your right and reach the entrance
to Wolvesey Castle and the Old Bishop's Palace (where Mary
Tudor first met Philip of Spain). Turn left along College Walk
and bear left with this road to cross Wharf Bridge.

3. Turn right along a road and soon bear right with the sign-
posted Itchen Way. Cross a bridge to continue with the river
on your left. Turn left over Tun Bridge and go right to walk
with the river, or its disused medieval canalised stretch, on
your right.

4. Turn left through a gate to cross the grassed-over former A33
and enter St Catherine's Hill (Hampshire Wildlife Trust).
Bear left with the path up St Catherine's Hill to find the maze
near the beech trees at the summit.

5. Retrace your steps down St Catherine's Hill and go left with
the Itchen Navigation on your right. Pass under an old railway bridge and approach the din of the road on your left.

6. Turn right, away from the road, to go through gates and along
a lane. Cross a bridge over the River Itchen and turn right
along a private road sign-posted as a public footpath. Pass the
back of an old mill on your right and continue upstream with
the river on your right. Divert left to the Hospital of St Cross.

7. Resume walking upstream with the river on your right. Your
path is now part of the waymarked Clarendon Way. Turn
right at a road to cross a bridge and turn left to walk with the
playing fields of Winchester College across one channel of
the river on your left (the main river is on your right). Bear

right past Winchester College and go left with College Walk towards Wolvesey Castle. Turn left along College Street.

**8.** Turn right along the sign-posted route to the High Street which passes the west door of the cathedral. Go left to retrace your steps to the railway station.

# 13. Tichborne

**Route:**   Cheriton – Gander Down – Tichborne – Cheriton

**Distance:** 7 miles. Moderate.

**Maps:**    O.S. Pathfinders 1243 Winchester North & New Alresford and 1264 Winchester South, O.S. Landranger 185 Winchester & Basingstoke.

**Start:**   Cheriton parish hall (SU 583285).

**Access:**  Bus no 67 runs to Cheriton from Winchester and Petersfield.

## Curses Fulfilled

Every Lady Day (March 25) the head of the Tichborne family distributes a dole of flour to all the parishioners of Tichborne and Cheriton. This is done from the porch of the house, which dates from 1803. There was a house here in the 13th century, lived in by the same family, when Lady Mabella, Sir Roger Tichborne's wife, made a death-bed request that her husband should grant land to be used to provide the poor folk with a dole of bread. Meanly, he agreed to give the land his wife could walk around in the time it took for a brand to burn on the fire, the dying Lady Mabella managed to crawl around 23 acres, now known as 'The Crawls', north of Tichborne Park and beside the road to Alresford. Before she died, Lady Mabella laid a curse to discourage her descendants from any thoughts of discontinuing this dole. The curse did come about exactly as prescribed when the dole was suspended in 1796 because it was attracting unsavoury elements from elsewhere. The old house fell down, causing the new build-

HEERE LYETH RICHARD TICHBORNE Ý SONNE
OF SʳRICHARD TICHBORNE KNIGHT & DAME
SVSAN HIS WIFE ONE OF Ý DAVGHTERS &
COHEIRES OF Wᵐ WALLER ESQ WHOE DEPAR-
TED THIS LIFE Ý FIVETH DAY OF MARCH 1619
AFTER HE HAD LIVED ONE YEARE SIX
MONETHES & TOO DAIES

The memorial to the infant Richard Tichborne

ing to be erected, while Sir Henry Tichborne, the baronet at the
time, produced seven sons, then his eldest son had seven daugh-
ters. Sir Henry's third son, Edward, unexpectedly succeeded to
the baronetcy in 1826. He had earlier changed his name to
Doughty, in order to comply with the terms of a relative's will.
The family name was eclipsed, but this was trivial compared
with what was to follow. The title and the estates should have de-
scended to a Roger Tichborne, who was born in 1829. He was reported drowned off the coast of South America in 1854. His
mother couldn't accept her son's fate and advertised a reward for
his discovery. This prompted a situation that could step out of a
novel by Madeleine Brent. A ridiculously fat and old 'son' appeared to claim his inheritance. Other members of the family had
to endure the distraught mother being possessed by the curse into
recognising the impostor. The mysterious claimant even had the

support of a reputable local, to the bemusement of others. Once evil is abroad, the corruption becomes infectious. After 103 days, the claimant lost a civil law suit to gain the Tichborne inheritance. He was then found guilty of perjury after the longest trial ever held in this country, lasting 10 months. Arthur Orton, the son of a Wapping butcher, was eventually sentenced to 14 years in gaol. When in St Andrew's Church, buy the booklet about Tichborne's history and compare the photographs of Sir Anthony Doughty-Tichborne, 14th baronet, and the Tichborne Claimant and look closely at their eyes, nose and mouth.

The Tichborne family seems to collect curses in connection with providing food for the hungry. In 1619. Sir Richard Tichborne was in residence when a gypsy who had called at the house for sustenance was turned away. She cursed Sir Richard's infant son, also named Richard, naming the day he would die from drowning. That day the boy was taken, for safety, to the height of Gander Down, safely away from the River Itchen. Of course, the one year-old child went and drowned himself in a puddle in a cart-track! His memorial can be seen in the family's Roman Catholic chapel which occupies the north aisle of the Anglican church, by special permission of King James I to his most loyal, if Roman Catholic, subject, Sir Benjamin Tichborne. The Tichborne Dole has been restored, although parishioners now receive it in the form of flour.

## The Walk

*1.* With your back to Cheriton parish hall, go left and turn left along the access lane to the Church of St Michael and All Angels. Enter the churchyard and go right to walk with the wall on your right and pass the east end of the church on your left. Leave the churchyard by a kissing-gate and go left to head for a stile giving access to a children's playground. Cross this and immediately turn right over another stile. Go ahead along the sign-posted official diversion of the footpath, following the right-hand edge of this field and turning left in the corner

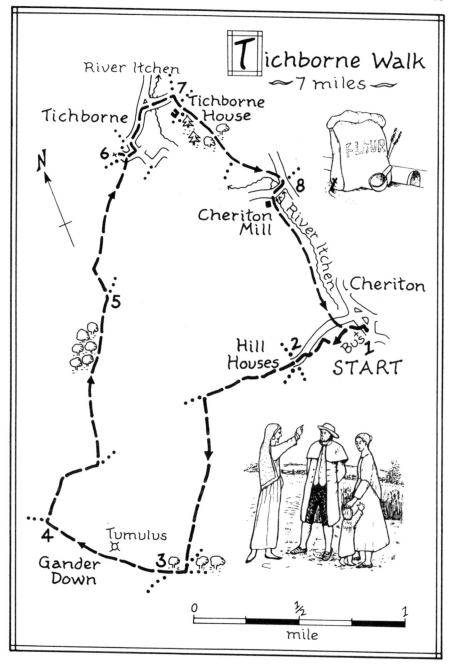

# **T**ichborne Walk
## ～7 miles～

River Itchen

7

Tichborne House

Tichborne

N

6

FLOUR

8

Cheriton Mill

River Itchen

Cheriton

5

Hill Houses

2

Bus 1

START

4

Tumulus

3

Gander Down

0        ½        1
mile

ahead. Bear right through a gate beside a signpost to reach a lane.

2. Go left along the lane. Ignore a sign-posted path going right and another forking left. Keep ahead with the lane whose surface deteriorates after Hill Houses. Turn left at a track junction. Follow this fenced track through a belt of trees and bear right to emerge through a gate.

3. Ignoring the waymarked bridleway which forks left, go straight ahead with the fence on your right. Continue through a gate beside a signpost, notice a tumulus on your right in the next field and bear very slightly left. Pass under power lines and take a gate ahead to follow a hedged track over Gander Down.

4. Reach a barn on your left and turn right along a waymarked bridleway, walking with a hedge on your right. Bear right through a gate in the corner of this field. When the hedge on your left turns away to form a corner, turn left to it and walk with the hedge on your left. Continue along a hedged track, pass woodland on your left, a barn on your right and a barn on your left.

5. 40 metres after the barn on your left, bear left over a stile and climb a sloping field to cross a stile in its top hedge. Turn right to walk beside a hedge on your right. Reach a lane and turn left to visit St Andrew's Church, Tichborne.

6. Go down the lane from the church to the road in Tichborne. Turn left along the road, which soon bends right to pass the Tichborne Arms pub on your right. Fork right along the private road to Tichborne Pottery.

7. Turn right after the pottery, approach the gates across the drive to Tichborne House and turn left over a stile. Turn right immediately to walk with a fence on your right. Continue over a stile beside a gate in the corner. Emerge from a belt of

woodland and go through a field. Cross a stile and bear left down to a road. Go right along this to a junction.

8. Turn right at the junction and turn left to pass Cheriton Mill by taking the sign-posted Wayfarer's Walk. Go upstream above the River Itchen on your left. Continue over stiles and along a fenced path. Cross a lane and bear left back to Cheriton church to retrace your steps to the bus stop outside the parish hall.

# 14. Selborne

**Route:**     Selborne – Wishing Stone – Selborne Common – Selborne

**Distance:** 3½ miles. Strenuous.

**Maps:**      O.S. Pathfinder 1244 Alton, O.S. Landranger 186 Aldershot & Guildford.

**Start:**      Selborne Arms, Selborne (SU 742335).

**Access:**    Selborne is served by bus no 54A from Alton and Portsmouth on Sundays and Public Holidays and bus no 72 from Alton and Petersfield on weekdays.

## Selborne's Wishing Stone

Selborne is one of those special spots which will draw those who are sensitive to the spirit of the land back to it again and again. The chief channel for this spirit in the eighteenth century was the naturalist and antiquary Gilbert White (1720-93). His letters to Daines Barrington and Thomas Pennant were published as a book by White's brother Benjamin in 1789. 'The Natural History and Antiquities of Selborne' became a classic. Find out more about its author at the museum in his old home at The Wakes. Visit its garden to trace the line of an old path which has been re-discovered by dowsing. It would appear to mark a ley or spirit path running between St Mary's Church, where Gilbert White spent much of his life as its curate and is now buried in the fifth grave from the outer north wall of the chancel and which boasted a fine old yew tree until very recently, and the early ecologist's most mysterious memorial. Gilbert and his brothers dragged a stone from nearby Farringdon and erected it at the top of Hanger Hill. The path known as the Zigzag was painstakingly cut by Gilbert and gives access to this stone, which marks where leys cross. Did he know about leys, or was he just so close to the earth that he was led to mark this sacred spot by instinct? The gallows tree stood nearby, emphasising the sacrificial nature of the spot. Tradition dictates, perhaps for good reason, that those who climb the zigzag should touch the stone and make a wish. Look northeastwards over the village to the site of a medieval priory at Priory Farm (SU 756345). A track whose surface was laid by the monks still connects this site with the church. Ghosts of the monks are seen from time to time.

## The Walk

**1.** Face the Selborne Arms pub and go left. Immediately turn right, as sign-posted for Hangers Way. Follow this footpath to Selborne Common (National Trust) and climb the zigzag Path to the Wishing Stone at its top.

**2.** With your back to your view over Selborne, take the woodland path ahead (not the path going right). When this grassy track over the Common forks, bear right to see a dew pond known to Gilbert White.

**3.** Retrace your steps to the fork and this time turn sharply right, as if forking left first time. Reach the sign-posted junction of your footpath with a bridleway.

**4.** Turn right to follow the bridleway inside the wood, keeping close to the perimeter on your left. Reach a stile on your left, but don't take it. Turn right with the woodland path.

5. Bear left, as waymarked by a blue arrow on a post. Keep near the edge of the wood on your left and above a wooded slope on your right. Emerge at a field and go right to walk with a field on your left, with the wood on your right.

6. Turn right along the lane to Selborne. Turn right at a junction to reach the museum on your right before returning to the bus stops outside the Selborne Arms.

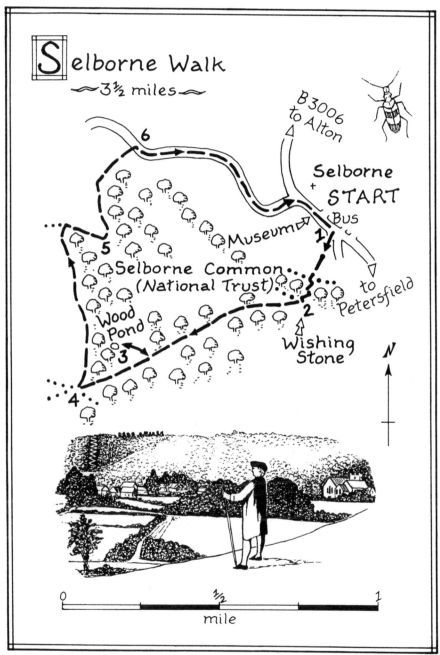

# Selborne Walk
~3½ miles~

6

B3006 to Alton

Selborne
START
Bus

Museum
1

5

Selborne Common
(National Trust)

to Petersfield

Wood Pond

2

3

Wishing Stone

4

N

0 ½ 1
mile

# 15. Telegraph Hill

**Route:**    Morestead – Deacon Hill – Telegraph Hill – Cheesefoot
             Head – Fawley Down – Morestead

**Distance:** 5 miles. Moderate.

**Maps:**    O.S. Pathfinder 1264 Winchester South, O.S.
             Landranger 185 Winchester & Basingstoke.

**Start:**   Bus shelter, Morestead (SU 509256).

**Access:**  Bus no 63 runs to Morestead from Winchester (tel.
             01256 464501 for details).

## Crop Circles and the Dragon's Tongue spits fire

Telegraph Hill contains the eye of the landscape figure of a
dragon (see Walk 20). Jane Whittle reckons the eye is formed by a
fir clump, but I would go for the nearby tumulus. If you think this
is too fanciful a creature, the path over Deacon Hill is subject to
closure when firing takes place at Chilcomb Ranges (Telephone
01962 853663 before setting out on this walk to check firing
times). This rifle range just happens to correspond to the dragon's
tongue. Well, a dragon's head must have its dangers!

   Enough people have had their fingers burnt by writing about
crop circles, but it's hard to avoid them in Hampshire. Yes, many
do seem to have been hoaxes, but there are others that remain
stubbornly genuine. A few have even been seen being made, including one formed by a flying saucer at Cheesefoot Head in the
summer of 1980. Three crop circles appeared within the Devil's
punchbowl, below Cheesefoot Head, in the summer of 1981. A
large circle was accompanied by two rings. Unlike later circles,

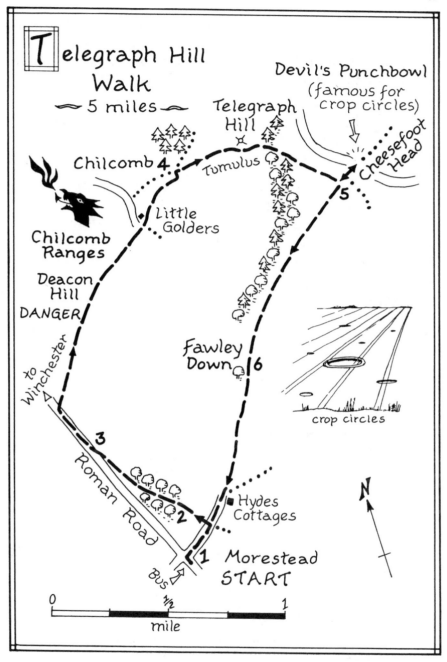

**Telegraph Hill Walk**
~ 5 miles ~

Devil's Punchbowl
(famous for crop circles)

Telegraph Hill

Cheesefoot Head

Chilcomb **4**

Tumulus

Little Golders

Chilcomb Ranges

Deacon Hill
DANGER

to Winchester

**5**

Fawley Down **6**

crop circles

**3**

Roman Road

**2**

Hydes Cottages

Bus

**1**   Morestead
START

0        ½        1
mile

N

there were no tractor tracks which would have allowed hoaxers access without leaving signs of their approach in the rest of the crop. The corn was also swirled in a clockwise direction and flattened without the damage expected of human feet.

Flying saucers seemed an obvious candidate for some people. Dr Terence Meaden presents a strong argument for whirlpools, or atmospheric vortices, in 'The Circles Effect and its Mysteries'. Interestingly, this would relate to a dream I recorded on the sacred peak of Carn Ingli in Wales, where such a vortex was seen in a dream involving the goddess Rhiannon's fingers and the stones of a stone circle. Such whirlwinds have even been witnessed creating crop circles in other parts of the country. Hopefully, the circles will keep appearing, allowing you to enjoy a view of them from Cheesefoot Head on a summer's day.

## The Walk

**DANGER! TELEPHONE 01962 853663** to find out when firing will take place at Chilcomb Ranges.

1. With your back to the bus shelter just south of the cross-roads on the northern edge of Morestead, turn left. With Hazeley Road on your left, turn right to climb with a lane. Reach a signpost marking where a right of way crosses this lane (it's a bridleway going right and a footpath going left). Turn left with the footpath to descend with a fence on your left.

2. Go ahead over stiles in the double fences in the corner and bear slightly left, as indicated by painted black arrows. Follow the path through the wooded slope, cross a track descending to the valley on your right and climb gradually to emerge on open downland. Go ahead to take a stile in the far left-hand corner and reach a road.

3. Go right along what was a Roman road (and one from the days of Molmutius around 500 BC). Turn right along a track signposted as a bridleway. Red flags or lamps will give warning of

firing on Chilcomb Ranges (the dragon's tongue, spitting fire!). If there is no firing, follow the hedged path to Little Golders, where you ignore the lane descending on your left. Continue along the hedged track.

Looking south-east from direction point 3

4. Pass a sign-posted path crossing a field on your left and ignore a hedged track forking left downhill. Bear right with a track that soon passes a wedge of trees on your right. Reach a tumulus at the top of Telegraph Hill (the eye of the dragon?).

5. Go ahead along a track to reach a path junction where a sign-post was erected in memory of Mike Heneghan. Divert left along the South Downs Way to the road at Cheesefoot Head to gain a view over the Devil's Punchbowl, famous for its crop circles. Retrace your steps to the memorial sign-posted junction and take the bridleway which is now ahead (it was on your right before diverting to Cheesefoot Head). Follow this grassy track over the open acres of Fawley Down.

6. Pass a small triangle of trees on your right. Follow the hedged track to a junction with a track coming sharply from your left at Hydes Cottages. Go ahead down the lane to Morestead.

# 16. Bokerley Ditch

**Route:**    Martin – Martin Down – Bokerley Ditch – Roman Road
                – Martin Drove End – Martin

**Distance:** 6½ miles. Easy.

**Maps:**     O.S. Pathfinders 1262 Salisbury (South) & Broad
                Chalke and 1282 Fordingbridge, O.S. Landranger 184
                Salisbury & The Plain.

**Start:**    If coming by bus no 42, the bus stop at Townsend Lane,
                Martin (SU 065199), if coming by bus no 184, the bus
                stop at Martin Drove End (SU 052210), if coming by
                car, the car park for Martin Down National Nature
                Reserve (SU 058192).

**Access:**   Bus no 42 comes to Martin (Townsend Lane) from
                Salisbury. There is a more frequent service to Martin
                Drove End by bus no 184 from Salisbury and
                Weymouth. Telephone 01722 336855 for details.

## Ancient Border

Bokerley Ditch is an impressive earthwork neatly dividing
Hampshire and Dorset. Why should two English counties merit
the sort of structure normally associated with the wild Welsh or
Scots? It is only four miles long because its function was to plug
the gap made by the Roman (pre-Roman?) road known as Ackling
Dyke, which connected Old Sarum with Badbury Rings. The
flanks of this road were covered by forest. The road passed by the
barrier in the early fourth century, but coins found dating from

the reign of Valens, who was emperor from 364 to 378, suggest that it was extended across the road then. A coin of Honorius (dating from 393) indicates when the road was unblocked, while the barrier may have become more permanent in the days of the Saxons. The Hampshire side of the Ditch is more formidable, suggesting that it was defended by Britons in Dorset, stemming the tide of Saxons coming from Hampshire. Pentridge, on the

Bokerley Ditch

Dorset side of the border, has a Celtic name and a church dedicated to a Celtic saint.

The longevity of this border is also indicated by a stretch of Bronze Age ditch crossing Martin Down and marked on the O.S. map as Grim's Ditch. Grim's name was given by the English to many ditches they couldn't understand the reason for in their new country. Grim refers to the Norse God Odin, who liked to conceal himself. Strange ditches were presumed to be his work.

Perhaps the most mysterious aspect of Bokerley Ditch is that it reflects civil discontent in Roman Britain. Perhaps it dates from the time of Carausius, an Irishman whose abilities led to him being appointed admiral of the fleet by the Romans. Realising how Rome neglected Britain, he proved himself an able statesmen when setting up an independent British state near the end of the third century. His son, Carausius II, reigned in the middle of the fourth century and was an ancestor of Vortigern and of Cerdic.

## The Walk

1. Starting from the car park at Martin Down National Nature Reserve, bear left with a track running with a hedge on your left. Almost immediately, fork right along a track which gradually ascends through downland to Bokerley Ditch.

2. Turn right to walk with the mighty earthworks on your left. Eventually meet the A354 road at a sign for Woodyates. Go left to reach a lay-by on your right.

3. Turn sharply right to take a sign-posted bridleway (the Roman road, Ackling Dyke) to a lane.

4. Turn right along the lane to cross the A354 where the no 184 bus stops at Martin Drove End. Go ahead along the road for Martin, passing Townsend Lane, where the no 42 bus stops, on your right.

5. Continue into Martin and turn right along Sillens Lane to reach the car park at Martin Down National Nature Reserve.

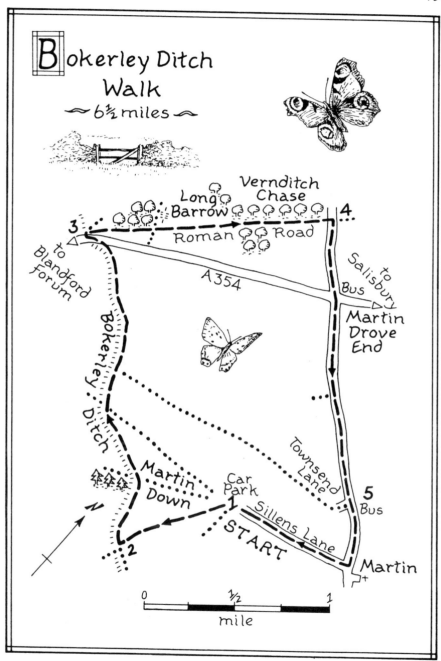

# Bokerley Ditch Walk
## ~ 6¾ miles ~

Vernditch Chase
Long Barrow
Roman Road
4
to Blandford Forum
to Salisbury
Bus
Martin Drove End
A354
3
Bokerley Ditch
Townsend Lane
Martin Down
Car Park
5
Bus
N
1
Sillens Lane
START
2
Martin

0  ½  1
mile

# 17. Breamore Mizmaze

**Route:**   Breamore – Breamore House – Mizmaze – Gallows Hill
– North Charford Down – Breamore Church –
Breamore

**Distance:** 7 miles. Moderate.

**Maps:**   O.S. Pathfinders 1262 Salisbury (South) & Broad
Chalke and 1282 Fordingbridge, O.S. Landranger 184
Salisbury & The Plain.

**Start:**   Breamore post office (SU 158180).

**Access:**  Bus no X3 connects Breamore with Salisbury and
Poole. Telephone 01722 336855 for details.

## An Amazing Place

Certain little roadside villages give the appearance to passing motorists of a quiet ordinariness that belies their true significance. It
awaits the pedestrian tourist to discover the greatness of the spirit
of the place. Forgetting the fine Elizabethan manor house (open
to the public from April to September), here is a maze in a sacred
grove, a giant's grave, a spirit path to a hill where people were put
to death, an old and interesting church and the site of a battle between Celt and Saxon.

Breamore Mizmaze is one of only eight intact ancient turf
mazes in England today. Nigel Pennick, author of 'Mazes and
Labyrinths', rates this as the 'most exceptional'. About 26 metres
in diameter, it represents the winding path of life. A local tradition, recorded by Jeff Saward in 'Caer Sidi', is that a man could
run from the maze to nearby Gallows Hill and back 'in the time it

The Anglo-Saxon inscription in St Mary's Church

would take another man to walk round the maze'. Persevere in following the maze and learn wisdom. Breamore's old Saxon church has an interesting old inscription stating in translation 'Here is made plain the covenant to thee' ('Her swutelath seo gecwydraednes the' in Anglo-Saxon).

There are two stories about the Giant's Grave near the Mizmaze (and a second Giant's Grave to the north at SU 161230). One says the giant is the Bevis linked also with Tangley (Walk 3) and Ports Down (see Walk 24). Another makes it the grave of Natan-Leod, the leader of the Britons who fought the Saxons here, at Charford (Cerdicsford) in 519. Some say 5000 Britons fell in this defeat. Others point out that Natan-Leod lived to fight another day and that the Saxons didn't succeed in gaining ground to the north until Cerdic's son took Old Sarum in 552. Natan-Leod we can take to be a local commander based in Winchester and, most probably, on the side of King Arthur. We can be more certain about Cerdic and dispel the notion that we are dealing with a Saxon invader. Cerdic is a British name, akin to Ceredig, Caradoc or Caractacus. A leader of the Gewissei (from whom we have the name Wessex – nothing to do with West Saxons), he was the son of Elesa, who was the Eliseg commemorated on Eliseg's Pillar near Llangollen in North Wales and the Elafius who welcomed St Germanus, Bishop of Auxerre. Germanus came to Britain in the fifth century on behalf of the pope to eradicate the Pelagian heresy, with its notions of karma and reincarnation. The title of Dux Gewissei was borne by the notorious Vortigern, who had gained it by marriage to Sevira, the daughter of Magnus Maximus and Elen. The expulsion of Elesa coincided with the overthrow of Vortigern by Ambrosius. The dispossessed Cerdic returned in 494 with Saxon allies and he succeeded in reclaiming what became Hampshire with the aid of Saxons and Jutes. Cerdic was British, however, while his descendants became Kings of Wessex and of England.

The ley followed by the path between the Mizmaze and Gallows Hill can be extended to the eastern edge of Frankenbury Camp (Walk 18).

## The Walk

1.  Face Breamore post office and go right. Turn left, as signposted for Breamore Church. Keep ahead as the road forks left. Pass a sign-posted footpath on your left. At a junction of four roads, bear right as sign-posted for Breamore Church.

2.  Continue along the drive sign-posted for Breamore House. Pass the house on your right and take a track through woodland ahead. Converge with a track coming from your right and go ahead with a hedged track. Emerge on open land and bear left to the Mizmaze (screened by trees, but signed).

3.  The Giant's Grave can be found on private land on the far side of the woodland enclosing the Mizmaze. Continue this walk along the track which leaves the wood and the maze on your left. Go ahead with a straight track, which is a ley from Frankenbury Camp, towards Gallows Hill. Go right to join another

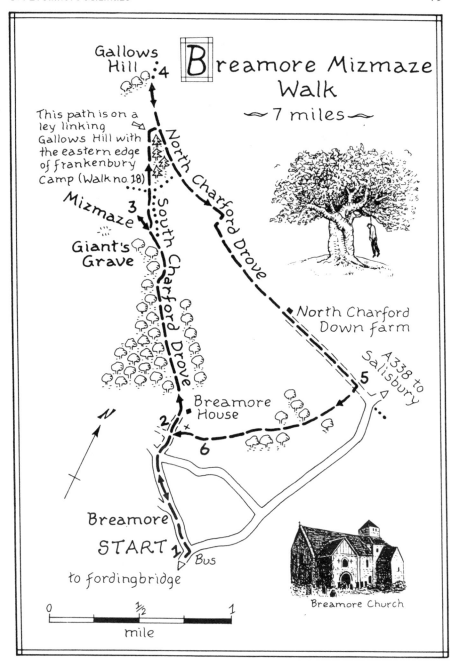

Gallows Hill :4

**B**reamore Mizmaze Walk
~7 miles~

This path is on a
ley linking
Gallows Hill with
the eastern edge
of frankenbury
Camp (Walk no. 18)

North Charford Drove

Mizmaze 3

South Charford Drove

Giant's Grave

North Charford Down farm

A338 to Salisbury

5

Breamore House

2

6

N

Breamore
START 1
Bus
to fordingbridge

Breamore Church

0       1/2       1
mile

track coming from your right and go left with it to Gallows Hill, where trees cover the tumuli.

4. Retrace your steps to the path junction. This time, take the hedged track straight ahead, being North Charford Drove. Follow this almost to the main road.

5. Turn right to walk with a track running parallel to the main road and at one field's distance from it, on your left. Go ahead through a kissing-gate and along the left-hand edge of a field. Pass woodland on your left, cross a stile beside a gate ahead to continue with a fence on your right. Go ahead over another stile.

6. Take a gate on your right in the next corner and cross a field to St Mary's Church, Breamore. Bear left along the lane to retrace your steps to the village post office and the bus stops.

# 18. Frankenbury Camp

**Route:** Burgate Cross – Lower Burgate – Frankenbury Camp – Lower Burgate – Burgate Cross

**Distance:** 4½ miles. Moderate.

**Maps:** O.S. Pathfinder 1282 Fordingbridge, O.S. Landranger 184 Salisbury & The Plain.

**Start:** Burgate Cross (SU 154164).

**Access:** Bus no X3 runs to Burgate Cross from Salisbury and Poole. Telephone 01722 336855 for details.

## A Famous Ley

The ley running nearly north-south through Stonehenge, Old Sarum, Salisbury Cathedral and Clearbury Ring is a classic. Read more about it in Walks in Mysterious Wiltshire. Hampshire can lay claim to it too, however. As Paul Devereux and Ian Thomson show in their 'The Ley Hunter's Companion', it extends to glance the western edge of Frankenbury Camp. It is typical of leys to strike the rim of Iron Age hillforts. Devereux and Thomson also note the sighting of UFOs or strange lights in the sky in this area. Paul Devereux's 'Earth Lights Revelation' deals more with this phenomena, associated with the spirit of the living earth. G.J. Harris has recorded further research on this alignment in The Ley Hunter no 107, extending it southwards across Huckles Brook Bridge, Linford Brook Bridge, six boundary stones, a mound and a barrow on Kingston Great Common and reaching the sea at Highcliffe Castle.

Frankenbury Camp has another ley clipping its eastern edge and coming from Gallows Hill (see Walk 17). For the record, I dowsed leys at 120 degrees (124 minus 4 for magnetic variation) and 16 degrees (20 minus 4) at Burgate Cross. This may mark where male and female lines meet, as written about by Hamish Miller and Paul Broadhurst in 'The Sun and the Serpent'.

## The Walk

1. Walk south to pass the cross on your right. Pass the sign-posted Avon Valley Path (Christchurch 20 miles) on your right, then the Tudor Rose Inn on your right.

2. Turn left with the sign-posted Avon Valley Path (Salisbury 14 miles) and pass a farmyard. Bear left, as sign-posted, to cross a foot-bridge over the Avon. Go ahead through meadow, cross another foot-bridge and bear right. Continue over three more footbridges and along a fenced track towards the wooded slope on the far side of this valley.

Cross this stile to enter the woodland surrounding Frankenbury Camp

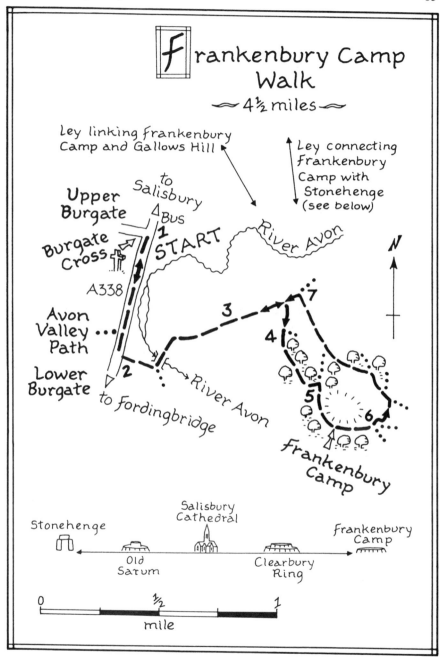

# ƒrankenbury Camp Walk
## ～4½ miles～

Ley linking ƒrankenbury Camp and Gallows Hill ►

Ley connecting ƒrankenbury Camp with Stonehenge (see below)

Upper Burgate

to Salisbury

△Bus

Burgate Cross

START

River Avon

N

A338

Avon Valley Path

3

7

4

Lower Burgate

2

River Avon

to ƒordingbridge

5

6

ƒrankenbury Camp

Stonehenge

Salisbury Cathedral

ƒrankenbury Camp

Old Sarum

Clearbury Ring

0                    ½                    1
mile

3.  Go ahead over a stile beside a gate then two bridges over water channels. Follow the hedged track to a junction with a sign-posted track on your right. Turn right over a stile to follow another track.

4.  Fork right, as sign-posted, down a woodland path and along the foot of the wooded slope. Emerge over a stile beside a gate to bear left through a field to a stile giving access to woodland.

5.  Take the waymarked path up the wooded slope and turn right at the top (don't take the stile in the fence ahead!). Follow the path around the western edge of Frankenbury Camp, on your left.

6.  Turn left over a stile and walk along the right-hand edge of a field. A stile in the corner ahead gives access to a hedged track. Turn left along this, bearing left at a house passed on your right. Pass a sign-posted path into woods on your right.

7.  Turn left at a signpost in a farmyard to take a gate and follow a hedged track to rejoin your outward route. Retrace your steps to the start, or catch a bus from a stop at Lower Burgate.

# 19. Marwell Hall

**Route:**     Owslebury – Marwell – Owslebury

**Distance:** 4 miles. Moderate.

**Maps:**     O.S. Pathfinder 1264 Winchester South, O.S. Landranger 185 Winchester & Basingstoke.

**Start:**     The Ship Inn, Owslebury (SU 511233).

**Access:**  Bus no 63 runs to Owslebury from Winchester (tel. 01256 464501 for details).

## The Mistletoe Bride

Marwell Hall's history would lead one to expect a ghost or two. Jane Seymour is said to have married Henry VIII here as soon as the king was sure that Anne Boleyn had been executed, in 1536. The fact is that the property was not in her family's possession till after the wedding. When it was, Sir Henry Seymour was cursed by the local priest and this curse seems to cover all owners of the hall (now a Preservation Trust). Perhaps it was responsible for the tragedy of the 'Mistletoe Bride', the subject of a ballad by Thomas Haynes Bayley in the 19th century:

'...an oak chest that had long lain hid, Was found in the castle, they raised the lid, And a skeleton form lay mouldering there, In the bridal wreath of the lady fair.'

A young bride, weary of dancing and partial to a game of hide-and-seek on the night of her Christmastide wedding, hid herself in an old oak chest. Too late, she discovered that the spring-lock would not permit her escape and that the heavy chest muffled her

cries for help. When
her body was discov-
ered many years
later, a sprig of mis-
tletoe was by her
side. The ballad re-
fers to Christmas Eve,
but it is said that
around 11pm on Box-
ing Day the sounds of
the crowd of young
wedding guests can
be heard rushing
along the corridors of
Marwell Hall. Proof
of the story was a
chest that was kept in
the hall until the
1850s, then in the
rectory at nearby
Upham. It has now
vanished.

The old hedged track to Owslebury

## The Walk

*1.* With the Ship Inn on your left, take the road through Owslebury. Bear right along a path through the churchyard, passing
the church on your right.

*2.* Go right down a lane sign-posted as a footpath. This becomes
a hedged track from which you emerge into the corner of a
field. Turn right to walk beside a hedge on your right. Reach a
corner where you turn left to go down the field beside a hedge
on your right.

*3.* Turn right in the bottom corner to keep walking with a hedge
on your right. Turn left in the next corner to climb beside a

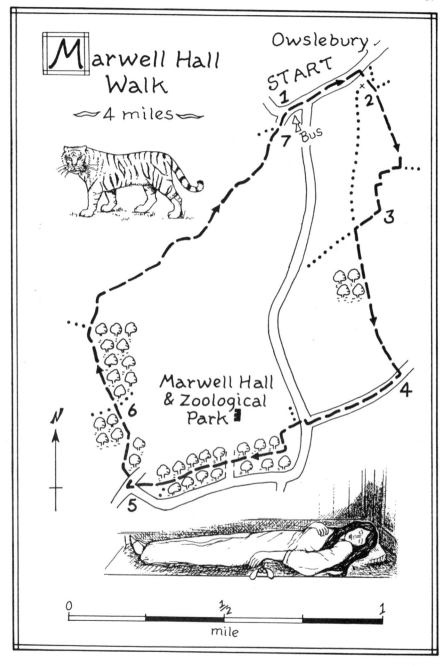

hedge on your right. Pass a patch of woodland on your right and go ahead to reach a road.

4. Go right to a road junction. Turn right for 30 metres, then turn left along a sign-posted bridleway, passing the zoological park behind a fence on your right. Turn left with this fence. Go right along a woodland path, with views of Marwell Hall away to your right. Cross an access lane, continue with the woodland path and fork right to emerge at a roadside bridleway signpost.

5. Go right to take a sign-posted bridleway which passes the entrance to the zoo on your right. Go ahead through more woodland.

6. Pass a waymarked bridleway on your left and a footpath on your right. Pass woodland on your right, then bear right at a fork to walk with a field on the other side of the hedge on your left, with young trees planted in the space on your right.

7. Converge with a sign-posted footpath coming sharply from your left. Go right to emerge at a road. Go right to reach Owslebury's Ship Inn on your left and the bus terminus on your right.

# 20. Old Winchester Hill

**Route:**    West Meon – Old Winchester Hill – West Meon

**Distance:** 6 miles. Strenuous.

**Maps:**    O.S. Pathfinder 1265 Petersfield & the Meon Valley,
             O.S. Landranger 185 Winchester & Basingstoke.

**Start:**    The Thomas Lord Inn, West Meon (SU 643240).

**Access:**   Buses nos 52 (Southampton – Petersfield) and 67
             (Winchester – Petersfield) stop at the Thomas Lord Inn,
             West Meon.

## The Dragon's Tail

Was there a link between Old Winchester Hill and modern Winchester? Perhaps this Iron Age camp occupied a site of comparable importance to the capital city of Wessex. It was certainly an important Bronze Age cemetery, including a circular depression which is a rare pond barrow. There is a ley or spirit path going through the trig point at the summit and the bowl-barrow immediately to the west of it at a bearing of 298 degrees (302 minus 4 degrees for magnetic variation). This ley clips the southern end of the northern barrow below the western rampart, continues through the western of two tumuli on Beacon Hill and another tumulus at SU 576242 on its way to Winchester Cathedral, which occupies an ancient sacred site.

Somerset has its Glastonbury Zodiac, whose giant landscape figures have been detailed by Mary Caine. This part of Hampshire has a dragon in its landscape, perceived by Jane Whittle, author of 'Twenty Wessex Walks'. With its nose at St Catherine's Hill

The trig point on Old Winchester Hill

(Walk 12) and its eye on Telegraph Hill (Walk 15), this dragon has its tail coiled around the prehistoric fort on Old Winchester Hill. The dragon symbolises the dark, lunar, feminine principle, where intuition reigns over logic and chaos over order. As the rhythm of life it joins earth and sky, moon and sun, body and spirit.

## The Walk

1.  With your back to the Thomas Lord Inn, go right to pass the bus shelter and telephone box on your right. Bear left at a road junction. Pass the Red Lion Inn on your right. Turn left at Station Road. Follow this road across the bridge over the course of the dismantled railway and continue uphill.

2.  Go left at a road junction. Ignore the sign-posted South Downs Way which bears left. Reach a car park on your right and take a gate at its rear to enter Old Winchester Hill Na-

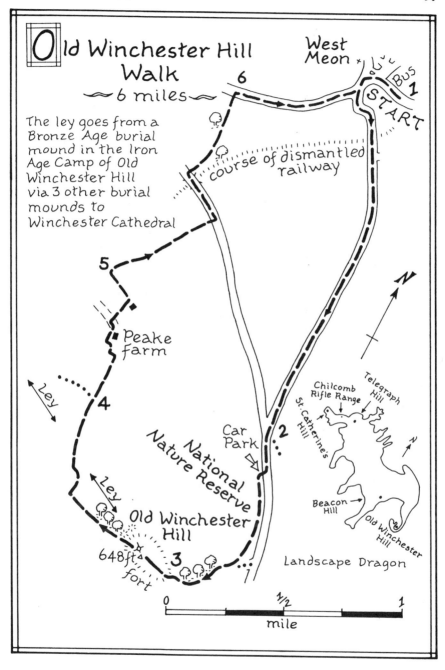

# Old Winchester Hill Walk
## ~ 6 miles ~

The ley goes from a
Bronze Age burial
mound in the Iron
Age Camp of Old
Winchester Hill
via 3 other burial
mounds to
Winchester Cathedral

West Meon

BUS

START

6

5

Peake Farm

Ley

4

course of dismantled railway

Ley

Old Winchester Hill

648ft fort

3

Car Park

National Nature Reserve

2

1

Chilcomb Rifle Range

Telegraph Hill

St. Catherine's Hill

Beacon Hill

Old Winchester Hill

Landscape Dragon

N

0    ½    1
mile

tional Nature Reserve. Bear left along the downland (NB. Do not stray from the path because of unexploded bombs!). Join a track going right to reach Old Winchester Hill Iron Age fort.

**3.** Follow the path through the centre of the hillfort, passing the trig. point at the 648 ft summit, through which runs the ley to Winchester Cathedral. Descend with the path to cross a stile beside a gate and pass woodland on your right. Continue out of the National Nature Reserve along a fenced path which turns right in the next corner, then bears left and turns right to reach a sign-posted junction.

**4.** Leave the South Downs Way to go left while you take the concrete lane straight ahead. As the lane bends right on the final approach to Peake Farm, take a gate in the corner on your left and turn right along the sign-posted official path diversion. This passes the farm buildings on your right. Go left along a lane for 50 metres, then turn right along the right-hand edge of a field, cross a footbridge in the corner and turn left, as sign-posted, along a track.

**5.** Turn right with the track and reach a road. Go left to cross a bridge over the dismantled railway. Turn right along a sign-posted footpath to walk above the old railway cutting. Bear left over a stile and take a delightful woodland path through a belt of beech trees.

**6.** Turn right along a road to return to West Meon.

# 21. Hambledon

**Route:**     Hambledon – Vineyard – Modern Cricket Ground – Bat
and Ball Inn – Broadhalfpenny Down – Hambledon

**Distance:** 6½ miles. Moderate.

**Maps:**      O.S. Pathfinder 1285 Horndean, O.S. Landrangers
185 Winchester & Basingstoke and 196 The Solent.

**Start:**     The Vine Inn, Hambledon (SU 645150).

**Access:**   Bus no 45 runs to Hambledon from Portsmouth.

## The Cradle of Cricket

Foreigners usually find the game of cricket one of the most mysterious features of English life. It is probably full of mystical symbols and paying homage to the Goddess (in which other game could you bowl a maiden over?). Shepherds are said to have played a version of cricket on the downs of Kent, Sussex and Hampshire for centuries. Here on Broadhalfpenny Down is the most historic cricket ground in the world, preceding Lord's.

Broadhalfpenny refers to the toll for booths at fairs held on this down – a right granted by James I to the Bishop of Winchester in 1612. It became the 'cradle of cricket' with the village cricket team beating the Rest of England 29 times out of 51 matches played between 1772 and 1781. One match, played on 18 June, 1777, and won by Hambledon by an innings and 168 runs, was played for the huge sum of 1000 guineas. The players wore sky blue coats (when not in the field), white shirts and breeches, stockings, gold-laced tricorne hats (but dark velvet caps when playing), plus buckle shoes.

Richard Nyren, landlord of the Bat and Ball Inn, was captain, secretary, groundsman and rule-maker. He put the game on a firm organised basis, formulated the rules, promoted the growth of club cricket and his authority was generally accepted. The club broke up when Richard Nyren left Hambledon in 1791, four years after the formation of the Marylebone Cricket Club in London saw the control and administration of the game move to the capital. See the bat presented to the departing Richard Nyren in 1791, now kept in the Bat and Ball Inn, plus the granite obelisk marking the site of the original ground, opposite the pub. Matches are still played there, including in the middle of winter on occasions. The village cricket team now plays at a ground passed by this route near Park Farm, between Broadhalfpenny Down and Windmill Down. Richard Nyren is known to have moved the ground to Windmill Hill, passed after you walk through the vineyard, in 1782, when he moved from the Bat and Ball Inn to the George Hotel in the centre of the village. Cricket lovers from all over the world, including Life Members in Australia, South Africa, Malawi, Zambia, the USA and the Netherlands, contributed to the

The Bat and Ball Inn, Hambledon

building of a new pavilion at the modern village cricket club ground in 1969.

The spirit of fair play was extended to the fugitive King Charles II when he came this way in 1651, fleeing to France after his defeat at Worcester. 'The Hambledon Boys' are known to have fought on the Roundhead side, but Charles, disguised as a poor yeoman, was sheltered in a cottage at Hambledon before reaching the coast and exile.

## The Walk

1.  Face The Vine Inn and go right. Pass a telephone box and The Gardens on your left. Turn left up a No Through Road and look for a narrow path leading right from this to the church of SS Peter and Paul. Take the path through the churchyard, passing the church on your left. Cross a road to take a lane which passes the infant school on your left. Continue along an enclosed footpath waymarked as part of the Wayfarer's Walk. Go past a vineyard and turn left up a track waymarked as a path.

2.  Turn right over a stile to walk along the lower slope of Windmill Down. Cross a stile ahead and take the path through a field to a road.

3.  Cross the road to take a stile into the modern village cricket ground and walk, as sign-posted, along its right-hand edge. Continue past a belt of trees on your right, take a waymarked gap in the hedge ahead and go ahead, as sign-posted, through a field to a sign-posted path junction.

4.  Turn sharply right back through the same field towards woodland. Reach another signpost and turn sharply left to cross the field again! Turn right with the waymarked Wayfarer's Walk (a green arrow) to take the left-hand edge of this field.

5.  Bear left, as waymarked, into woodland, then along the right-hand edge of a field, passing the wood on your right. Reach a lane and take the gate opposite. Walk along the left-hand edge of a field, cross a stile in the corner and turn right to walk with a fence on your right. Turn right at a road and come to the Bat and Ball Inn, on your left, with the old cricket ground on your right.

6.  Bear right at the cross-roads, as sign-posted for Hambledon. Reach a junction with a road on your right and turn left over a stile to take a path which bears slightly right uphill. Cross a stile in the top fence and turn right along a track. Bear left with this track to Scotland Cottage and continue along its access lane.

7.  When the lane turns right, take a sign-posted track going left (part of the Wayfarer's Walk). Look for a waymarked stile on your left and turn right along a path through a field. Take a stile ahead to walk beside a fence on your left (ignore a stile in it), then bear right across a stile and a farm access lane to take a small wooden gate and follow a hedged path to a lane. Go right, but immediately forking left downhill to return to Hambledon, where you go left for the bus stop near The Vine Inn.

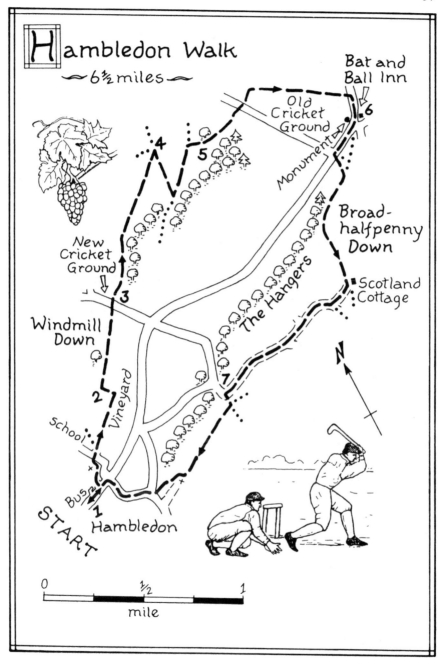

# Hambledon Walk
~ 6½ miles ~

Bat and Ball Inn

Old Cricket Ground

Monument

6

4

5

New Cricket Ground

Broad-halfpenny Down

Scotland Cottage

3

The Hangers

Windmill Down

Vineyard

2

7

School

Bus

1

START

Hambledon

N

0    ½    1
mile

# 22. William Rufus Stone

**Route:**    Brook – William Rufus Stone – Brook

**Distance:** 4 miles. Moderate.

**Maps:**     O.S. Outdoor Leisure 22 New Forest, O.S. Landranger
              195 Bournemoutn.

**Start:**    The Green Dragon Inn, Brook (SU 273141).

**Access:**   Buses nos 31 and 31A run to Brook from Southampton,
              although not all go as far as Brook (tel. 01202 673555).

## Why did William Rufus die?

The monument, a stone encased in iron to discourage vandalism,
records that this was the site of an oak tree on which an arrow
shot by Sir Walter Tyrrell at a stag glanced and struck King William II (William Rufus) on the breast, killing him instantly on
August 2, 1100. The corpse was laid on a cart belonging to a charcoal burner named Purkiss and taken for burial in Winchester Cathedral. The conventional view is that this was either an accident
or murder. It could have been an accident. Rufus' elder brother
Richard had died while still a youth, killed in a riding accident in
the New Forest. If that's what that was, of course. If an accident,
Sir Walter Tyrrell's arrow inflicted a fatal wound despite being
glanced off a tree, or a stag. It was an incredible bull's eye, straight
in the heart. Tyrrell also fled swiftly from the scene, crossing the
River Avon at a village now called Avon Tyrrell (SU 145990),
where a blacksmith reversed his horse's shoes in order to confuse
any pursuers. There were no pursuers and Tyrrell did not suffer
as a result of this accident. Perhaps he had taken the blame for

others – Tyrrell
protested his inno-
cence on his
death-bed. He was
a friend of Henry,
who succeeded
Rufus.

If William Rufus
was murdered, it
would most proba-
bly have been at
the behest of his
younger brother
Henry. Henry was
an ambitious man
who resented his
father's will. Wil-
liam the Con-
queror had
bestowed a fortune
on him, but no ter-
ritory. Robert be-
came Duke of
Normandy, while
William, known as
Rufus because of
his ruddy com-

KING WILLIAM
THE SECOND,
SURNAMED RUFUS
BEING SLAIN,
AS BEFORE RELATED,
WAS LAID IN A
CART, BELONGING
TO ONE PURKIS,
AND DRAWN FROM
HENCE, TO
WINCHESTER. AND
BURIED IN THE
CATHEDRAL CHURCH,
OF THAT CITY

The Rufus Stone

plexion (not his hair, which was blond), inherited the Kingdom
of England. While Tyrrell fled west to Poole and a ship to France,
Henry had rushed to Winchester, where he immediately claimed
the throne by right of his being born (after 1066) the son of a king.
His elder brother Robert was born only the son of a duke. Henry
was crowned hastily, on August 5, by the Bishop of London (there
wasn't time to summon an Archbishop). His brother Robert invaded England too late and withdrew when Henry promised to
pay an annual indemnity. Five years later, Henry ruthlessly

turned on his brother, keeping Robert a prisoner till he died in 1134, aged 80. Henry I made himself popular with his English subjects by marrying Eadgyth, or Edith, who became Queen Matilda. She was of royal Saxon descent and had been courted by Rufus. She had pretended to be a nun in order not to have to accept Rufus' proposal of marriage, so did Rufus die for the love of Matilda?

There is more to the death of Rufus, however. Margaret Murray hit the nail on the head in her book 'The Divine King in England'. Kingship involved being a channel for the Spirit of God, the Giver of Life. An unhealthy king would weaken his kingdom, necessitating the removal of the Spirit to a new, strong, body. The old king would be killed and the Spirit inducted into the new body in a solemn ceremony. The killing should take place at an interval of seven years. If the intended victim was still strong, he might have a substitute who would act as a king for a short spell before being killed in place of the king (as happened to Thomas a' Becket during the rein of the second Henry). William Rufus, whose name refers to the colour of life, was a pagan. He knew the need of a divine victim, especially in early August at Lughnasadh. His character was assassinated by Christian chroniclers, but he was actually a courageous servant to his people who accepted death without complaint.

Rufus was 42 (6 x 7 years) in the sacrificial month of August, 1100. He was also at the end of his second cycle of seven years as a king. After his first seven years he had arraigned Anselm on high treason, to provide a substitute. This time Rufus had to die. He spent his final hours smoothing the way for his successor, Henry, then drank more than usual before hunting. Rufus chose the two sharpest arrows for Tyrrell to fire. The king broke the shaft of the arrow when it projected from his body, fell upon the wound and accelerated his death. Known in Normandy within 24 hours, his death was expected, having been foretold in dreams, while the Abbot of Shrewsbury preached that 'the bow of God's vengeance is bent against the wicked. The arrow, swift to wound, is already drawn out of the quiver'. Of course, to the Church, Rufus was wicked. After all, he would leave sees empty in order to divert church funds into royal coffers. Even so, the Christian monk Ordaricus Vitalis wrote:

'Rufus was imperious, daring and warlike, and glorified in the pomp of his numerous troops. The king's memory was very tenacious, and his zeal for good or evil was ardent. Robbers and thieves felt the terrible weight of his power, and his efforts to keep the peace throughout his dominion were unceasing. He so managed his subjects, either by making them partakers of his bounty or curbing them by the terror of his arms, that no one dared whisper a word in opposition to his will.'

Here was a pagan king, doing his pagan duty. This extended to the way in which his corpse was carried to Winchester. The corpse of the king was left naked and unattended immediately after his death, symbolising that as he, naked and alone, received the Spirit of God, so he, naked and alone, resigned that Spirit. The sprinkling of his blood on the ground during the journey in the charcoal burner's cart was important. As Rufus' blood dripped from the corpse it revitalised the land. William Rufus was a Divine Victim.

Whatever the reason for William Rufus' death, it may not have been at this spot. The place names Fritham and Througham were probably confused and the correct spot may well be near Park Farm at SU 400967, not far from the Solent and, significantly, close to a chapel at St Leonard's Grange (William was said to have been killed near a chapel, which can't be found at Canterton). An ancient document refers to the Cistercian Abbey of Beaulieu being built near the spot where William Rufus was killed. Even so, the Rufus Stone must have been erected in this place for some special reason. Here are mysteries indeed!

## The Walk

*1.* With your back to the Green Dragon Inn, go right to take a footbridge over a stream. Fork right along Canterton Lane. This deteriorates to a stony track.

2. Turn right at a bridleway signpost to pass a house called Woodpecker on your left, then a house called Twin Oaks. Continue along a woodland track which becomes a lane running between hedgerows.

3. Turn left at a road junction and pass the Sir Walter Tyrrell Inn on your left. Continue to a car park on your left, opposite the Rufus Stone on your right.

4. Retrace your steps to the Sir Walter Tyrrell Inn, now on your right. Turn left through open pasture, keeping the forest on your right. Bear right to pass under telephone lines and take a sandy path which fords the stream known as Coalmeer Gutter.

5. Turn right to walk through a clearing between two parts of the New Forest. Cross one stream, go ahead and ford a broader stream known as King's Garn Gutter. Continue along a track which turns a corner on the right to reach a road.

6. Turn left along the road and emerge at a road junction in Brook. Go right to pass the Bell Inn on your left and reach the Green Dragon Inn on your right.

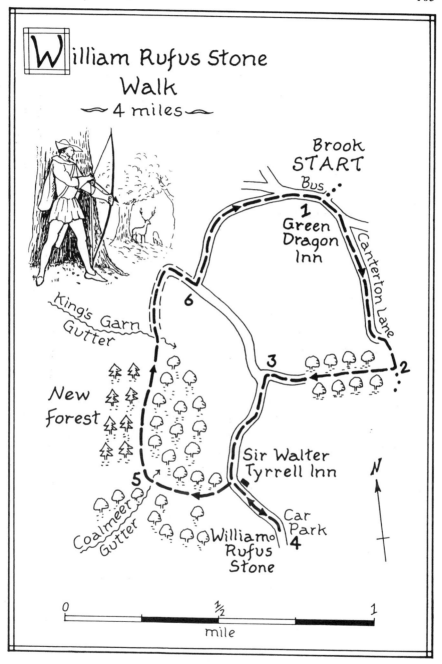

# William Rufus Stone Walk
## ~ 4 miles ~

Brook
**START**

Bus

**1**
Green
Dragon
Inn

Canterton Lane

King's Garn Gutter

**6**

New Forest

**3**

**2**

Sir Walter Tyrrell Inn

**N**

**5**

Coalmeer Gutter

William Rufus Stone

Car Park

**4**

0        ½        1
mile

# 23. The Bishop's Dyke

**Route:**     Beaulieu Road Station – Bishop's Dyke – Beaulieu
              Road Station

**Distance:** 4 miles. Moderate.

**Maps:**      O.S. Outdoor Leisure 22 New Forest, O.S. Landranger
              196 The Solent.

**Start:**     Beaulieu Road railway station (SU 349063).

**Access:**    Trains run to Beaulieu Road from London Waterloo,
              Southampton, Lymington Pier, Weymouth and
              Bournemouth.

## A Fat Bishop

The strange earthwork known as the Bishop's Dyke encloses an
area of about 202 hectares (500 acres) of poor, boggy ground. The
real mystery is why anybody should consider it valuable. Any-
way, the story is that around 1284, when Edward I was on the
throne (although one source does date it earlier, during King
John's reign), the Bishop of Winchester at the time was very fat.
This was probably John de Pontoise. It was the King's idea of a
joke to offer the Bishop a grant of 'as much land as he could crawl
around in one day'. The Bishop may have been fat, but he wasn't
stupid. He had a trolley made to support his huge stomach and he
ordered his monks to proceed ahead of him and make the way
easier as he propelled his trolley. It must have been quite a sight.

## The Walk

**1.** From the station, go right along the road to pass Beaulieu

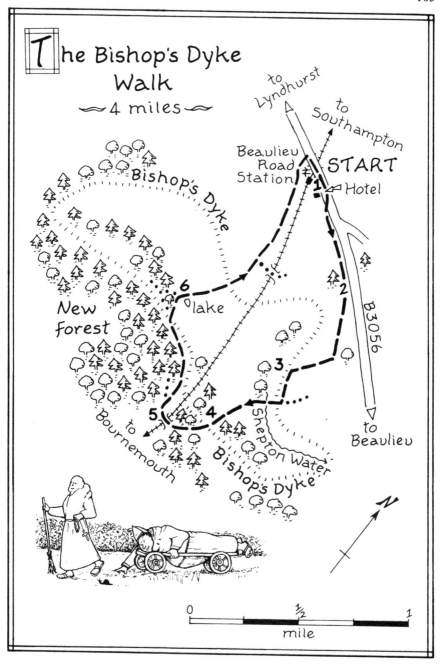

# The Bishop's Dyke Walk
## ~ 4 miles ~

to Lyndhurst

to Southampton

Beaulieu Road Station

START

Hotel

Bishop's Dyke

New Forest

lake

6

2

B3056

3

5

4

to Bournemouth

Shepton Water

Bishop's Dyke

to Beaulieu

N

0   ½   1

mile

Road Pub on your right and Beaulieu Hotel on your right. Walk on the heath parallel to the road on your left. Pass a junction with a road which bears left. Pass a clump of trees on your left, then a small patch of trees on your right.

2.  Bear right, away from the road, to follow a well-defined path to a line of trees on the horizon. Turn right at the trees to descend to the Bishop's Dyke, a linear earthwork.

3.  Go left to walk with the Bishop's Dyke on your right. When a broad path comes down from your left, turn right to take it and cross a footbridge and follow a boardwalk over wetland.

4.  Cross the Bishop's Dyke again and go ahead into woodland, bearing right with a grassy path to the railway and cross the bridge over the line.

5.  Follow the path as it bears right and passes the New Forest on your left. Bear right at a fork. Converge with a broad path coming from your left and go right.

6.  Cross a footbridge and follow the path as it bears slightly left, passing a bridge over the railway on your right. Go ahead to reach a road at a car park. Turn right for the railway station.

# 24. Portchester

**Route:**     Portchester railway station – Portchester Castle –
Portchester railway station

**Distance:** 3 miles. Easy.

**Maps:**     O.S. Pathfinder 1304 Portsmouth, O.S. Landranger
196 The Solent.

**Start:**      Portchester railway station (SU 617058).

**Access:**   Trains run to Portchester from Portsmouth and
Southampton. There are also local buses.

## Portchester

The impressive walls of Portchester Castle date from the Roman
era, although the Normans added the Keep in one corner. Built to
defend the shores of Britain from Saxons and to provide a naval
base from which ships would sail to deal with Saxon pirates, it is
associated with one of the most intriguing characters of Roman
Britain. Carausius was given command of the fleet during Dio-
cletian's reign, in AD 285. Evidence from coins suggest that Portchester Castle was built around this time, no doubt as a secure
base for a fleet anchored in Portsmouth Harbour. Its name was
probably Portus Adurni. Its walls and twenty bastions enclosed
an area of 3.4 hectares, where timber buildings conformed to a
grid of streets.

Given his command in Boulogne and thought by some to have
been a Belgian, Carausius may actually have been Irish. An able
statesman and warrior, he declared himself emperor in Britain in
286 and reigned until 293, when he was assassinated. The Ro-

Portchester Castle

mans eventually recaptured the province from his successor in 297 and, of course, Constantine the Great was yet to be born in York of a British mother and to make the Roman brand of Christianity the imperial religion. Carausius was clearly ahead of his time by trying to establish an independent British Empire. Some say that a contemporary ruler in Ireland, Cabri Lifeacher, was his brother. It does seem that Carausius established a dynasty in Britain and there is some debate as to whether a gravestone at Penmachno, in Gwynedd, is for Carausius or his son, referred to as Carausius II or Casnar Wledig. Carausius may have been Crair or Carawn of Menevia, the St David's area of Pembrokeshire, which has strong Irish connections. An interesting family line can be traced down from Casnar Wledig (Carausius II) through Erbin to Tewdrig, Meurig and the famous King Arthur of the early sixth century. So, the spirit of independence may have been alive and well in Britain during what an unconventional group of us consider to have been the dark days of the Roman Empire. The fort was occupied beyond the end of the Roman Empire and some think that it was here that in 501, according to The Anglo Saxon Chronicle, an indecisive battle was fought against invading Saxons or Jutes under the leadership of Port and his sons Bieda and Maegla. They came with two ships to a place called Portsa, seized land and slew a young British noble. No doubt such an event took place. Those who have linked it to the death of Sir Geraint, one of Arthur's knights, may be misplaced, however. Chris Barber would locate this in the Severn Estuary in his Journey to Avalon, while a personal favourite is Penbryn, north of Cardigan.

## The Walk

1.  From the railway station, go right along Station Road and take the subway to go ahead at a roundabout. Pass The Keep (a No Through Road) on your left.

2.  When level with Castle Primary School on your right, turn left along Cow Lane, a private road but public path. Fork right at a waste water pumping station and cross a stile to take the

enclosed path which goes over a series of stiles and emerges at a path junction.

**3.** Go ahead to pass swings on your left and walk with a hedge on your right. Approach the castle, bearing right along a path to a road and going left to the castle entrance.

**4.** Visit the castle and walk around the outside of its walls, anti-clockwise. Leave the castle on your left to take the shore path beside the sea on your right.

**5.** When the coastal bank bears right, turn left along a path through Castle Shore Park to return to the waste water pumping station. Bear right to retrace your steps to the railway station.

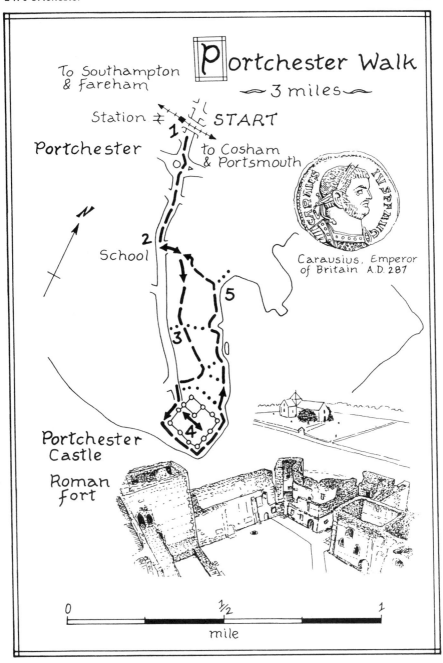

Portchester Walk
~3 miles~

To Southampton & Fareham

Station ⚇ START

Portchester

to Cosham & Portsmouth

1

School

2

N

5

3

Carausius, Emperor of Britain A.D. 287

4

Portchester Castle

Roman Fort

0    ½    1
mile

# 25. Burley

**Route:**     Burley – Castle Hill Fort – Smugglers Road – Burley
               Beacon – Shappen Hill – Burley

**Distance:** 6½ miles. Strenuous.

**Maps:**      O.S. Outdoor Leisure 22 New Forest, O.S. Landranger
               196 Bournemouth.

**Start:**     The Queen's Head Inn, Burley (SU 211031).

**Access:**    Bus no XI runs from Poole, Ringwood and
               Southampton to Burley, while buses nos 105 and 116
               connect Burley with Poole and Ringwood.

## Smugglers and Dragons

Step off the bus in Burley and you soon realise you are some-
where out of the ordinary. Shops have names like Witchcraft and
Witches Coven. No wonder the locals believed so strongly in free
trade that they became notorious for smuggling. Contraband was
carried from the sea at Highcliffe and taken past Burley on its way
to Salisbury. This exciting and illicit trade attracted a high-
spirited girl called Lovey Warne, who would parade on Vereley
Hill, north of Burley and visible from all directions. By dressing
in a bright scarlet cloak, she would give warning during daylight
of the presence of excisemen. The Smugglers used a sunken track
to avoid being seen, while the surrounding bracken could be used
for emergency cover. Markway Hill, traversed by the A35 east of
Burley at SU 243026, is a reminder of the risks taken by smugglers. A tree here was called the Naked Man after its use as a gallows.

Burley Beacon, on the ridge to the west of Burley, is an ancient beacon site with evidence of Bronze Age and Roman activity. Such a place is where leys radiate from and the untamed energy of this land may be behind a local legend. A dragon once lived on the beacon, descending to demand milk from the villagers. Eventually the good knight Sir Maurice de Berkeley set out to kill it. He left milk in cans and hid nearby. While the dragon was lapping up its daily pinta, Sir Maurice, accompanied by his two dogs, fell upon it. It must have been a fierce fight because the dogs perished, while Sir Maurice only survived because he had smeared himself with bird lime covered with powdered glass. Statues of the dogs can be seen on the terrace at Bisterne Park (SU 151007), while a dragon's head can be seen over the main entrance. The story comes from a document from Berkeley Castle, Gloucestershire, dating from before 1618 and accounting for the family's right to the land. The walk follows the course of the dismantled railway which used to link Brockenhurst with Broadstone. The original route between London and Poole came this way, which was known as 'Castleman's Corkscrew' after its chief promoter and because of its devious route. The line was closed in 1964.

## The Walk

**1.** With your back to the Queen's Head Inn, go right to the war memorial and fork right down Ringwood Road. Pass the entrance to Barley Manor Hotel on your right. Look for the sign-posted footpath 'Burley Street' and take it to walk above and to the right of the road as it rounds a bend. Go ahead at the end of this gated path, cross the road and join the pavement.

**2.** Turn left along a sign-posted footpath alongside the gated drive of Burley Hill House. Use the small gate to the right of the drive to take the fenced path. Follow the right of way through woodland on Burley Hill. Emerge over a stile beside a signpost onto a track.

**3.** Go right along the track to pass Blackbush Cottages. Enter the prehistoric fort on Castle Hill and bear left down a path to a road. Go left, passing a barrier on your left (note it for your return journey), cross a bridge and continue to a car park on your right -a Forestry Commission facility named 'Smugglers Road'.

4.  Go up the path at the back of the car park. Cross the ditch of the old Smugglers Road and bear right up a broad track. Turn right at a path junction to take a path back towards Castle Hill. Bear left at a fork.

5.  Descend to the road, go left and cross the bridge again. Reach the barrier on your right. This prevents cars from taking the track, but you can turn right along it, walking parallel to the wooded slope of Burley Hill, then the mysterious Burley Beacon, away to your left. Pass small, seasonal, ponds, before reaching a lake on your right. Continue along the track to reach a road at a car park.

6.  Go ahead past the car park on your right and join the course of a dismantled railway on your right. Bear left along this for one mile.

7.  Turn left along a track which takes a footbridge over a stream and bear slightly left up Shappen Hill to join a track coming from your right. Go left with this and turn right at the next track junction. Bear left downhill to a house and take a track ahead into woodland.

8.  Bear right at a junction with a lane serving the Moorhill House Hotel (on your left). Reach a car park and the bus stop for the no 105 and 116 services. Cross the road and turn left along the pavement back into Burley.

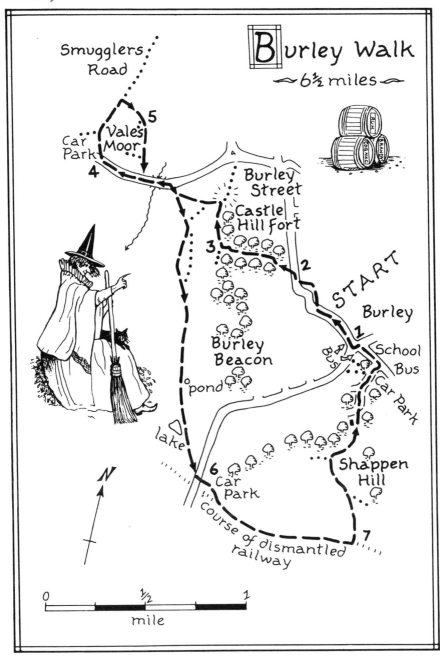

# Burley Walk

~ 6½ miles ~

Smugglers Road

5

Vale's Moor

Car Park

4

Burley Street

Castle Hill Fort

3

2

START

Burley

School Bus

Car Park

Bus

Burley Beacon

pond

Shappen Hill

lake

6

Car Park

N

course of dismantled railway

7

0   ½   1

mile

# 26. Beaulieu Abbey

**Route:**     Beaulieu – Buckler's Hard – Beaulieu

**Distance:** 5 miles. Easy.

**Maps:**     O.S. Outdoor Leisure 22 New Forest, O.S. Landranger
            196 The Solent.

**Start:**     Bus stop near the Abbey Church, Beaulieu (SU
            388024).

**Access:**   Bus no 123 runs to Beaulieu on Sundays, coming from
            Bournemouth via Lymington. Bus no 112 passes
            through Beaulieu on weekdays as it links Lymington
            with Hythe.

## Chanting Monks

The Abbey Church is a rare surviving building of the Cistercian
Abbey which was built on land granted by King John in 1204. It
was actually the Refectory and was converted into Beaulieu's
parish church after the Reformation. The old gatehouse became
the home of Lord Montagu's family and Beaulieu is now synony-
mous with vintage motor cars – the National Motor Museum is
housed here. For those of a supernatural disposition, Beaulieu
has many other attractions, it has many ghosts. Described as
kindly and gentle, they chant and perform masses for the dead.
When the Special Operations Executive used Beaulieu as a
training-base for secret agents, including Odette Churchill, during the second world war, some very tough people found them-
selves terrified at contact with the spirit world. The Cistercians
wore white, but the most notorious monk wears brown. He has

been seen holding a parchment or scroll and moves about gently on his ghostly business. The chanting usually precedes a death of a local person and seems to take the form of a requiem mass. Sometimes there is the strong smell of incense. The ghostly monks seem happy here, which shouldn't be surprising when you consider that they called this their 'beautiful place'.

The Maritime Museum at Buckler's Hard is well worth a visit to find out about what was a major shipbuilding centre in the days of Nelson. Visitors can also see the interiors of some houses in the village street, accurately recreated to show how labourers and shipwrights lived in the late eighteenth century. Buckler's Hard was also the home port of Gipsy Moth IV, in which Sir Francis Chichester sailed around the world in 1966, going 15,500 miles without putting into port. The film A Man For All Seasons was also made along this unspoilt river.

## The Walk

**1.** Face the Beaulieu River and go right to walk with the river on your left, leaving the Abbey Church on your right. Go ahead over a bridge and enter the village. Turn left just before the Montagu Arms Hotel, along the sign-posted Solent Way. Follow a gravel track as it bears right to a stile.

**2.** Go ahead over the stile and along the fenced track with the river across the field on your left. Continue over a stile beside a cattle grid and along a grassy (perhaps muddy) path with a fence on your left and a hedge on your right. Enter North Solent National Nature Reserve and follow the path across a stream.

**3.** Follow the firmly-surfaced and waymarked Solent Way up to the corner of a field and continue along its left-hand edge. Reach the next corner and take the lane sign-posted as a path to Buckler's Hard. Bear right at a lane junction and almost immediately turn left along a sign-posted path which takes you through woodland. Bear right after emerging from the wood, pass a marina on your left and come to the entrance to Buck-ler's Hard Yacht Harbour.

4. Bear slightly left along the sign-posted Riverside Walk. Pass moorings on your left and follow the track up to Buckler's Hard Maritime Museum (on your left at the top of the village street).

5. Retrace your steps to the start of the woodland track. Enter the wood, ignore a path going immediately to your right. Reach a sign-posted path junction.

6. Fork right to follow the alternative woodland path, nearer the river, on your right. This returns you to the main woodland track. Go right to retrace your steps to Beaulieu.

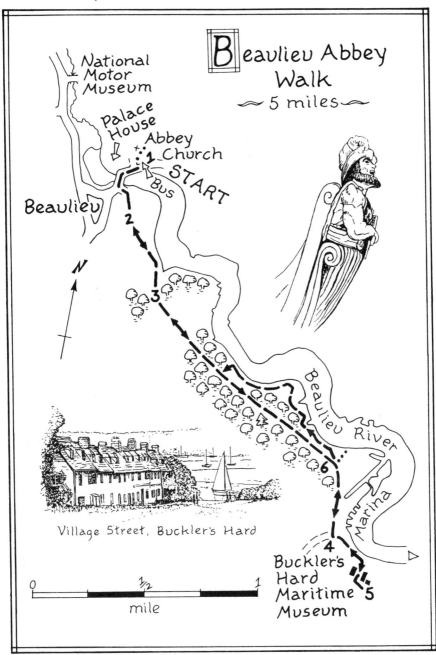

National Motor Museum

Palace House

Abbey Church

**B**eaulieu Abbey Walk
~ 5 miles ~

1 START

Bus

Beaulieu

2

N

3

Beaulieu River

6

4

Marina

5

Village Street, Buckler's Hard

Buckler's Hard Maritime Museum

0                    ½                    1
mile

# 27. Lepe

**Route:**     Bus terminus, Whitefield Farm, Langley – East Hill Farm – The Solent Shore – Lepe Country Park – Bus terminus, Whitefield Farm, Langley

**Distance:** 6 miles. Easy.

**Maps:**     O.S. Outdoor Leisure 22 New Forest, O.S. Landranger 196 The Solent.

**Start:**     Bus terminus, Whitefield Farm, Langley (SU 448006).

**Access:**     Bus no 38 from Southampton terminates at Whitefield Farm, Langley (N.B. not all services go as far as this – tel. 01703 226235). There is also a summer service (no x9) to Lepe Country Park.

## A Place to Leap from and to

The power of the word is strong, whatever the academic derivation of placenames. This stretch of the Solent's shore has been a place for making great leaps. In 1944 the direction was from here for France, when the hectic preparations for DD-Day included the construction of parts of the Mulberry harbours in the Beaulieu River just below Buckler's Hard, then their towing into position on Normandy's coast. Landing craft were also assembled here and the feverish activity was recorded by Nevil Shute in 'Requiem for a Wren'. There was a harbour at Lepe in Roman times, serving a road which was used by tin-traders from prehistoric times until the Middle Ages, when the Cornish tin trade still had its chief market in Southampton. The Isle of Wight, known to the Romans as Vectis, was probably the ancient Ictis (if you have

The shore path at high tide, west of Lepe

been brought up to believe that Ictis was St Michael's Mount in Cornwall, consider that the latter wasn't an island until after William the Conqueror's Domesday Survey). The tin was carried from Lepe to Gurnard, near Cowes, then taken across the Isle of Wight to Niton, where the Buddle Inn refers to a frame used to wash tin ore and there was most probably a port in Puckaster Cove. The Phoenicians may have sailed around the Iberian Peninsula from Cornwall, but the Jews and the Greeks would have preferred to sail from the Isle of Wight to the mouth of the River Seine, then along French rivers to Marseilles. Joseph of Arimathea may have come here, perhaps with the young Jesus.

The traffic was in the other direction around AD 495, when Cerdic, the founder of the Wessex dynasty which was to include Alfred the Great, landed here. Nearby Cadland House (SZ 468998) bears an interesting name, suggesting a battle. Cerdic's invasion has been seen as that of Saxons overcoming British resistance. Wessex has even been defined as the land of the West

Saxons. What seems much more likely is that Cerdic was a Briton and that Wessex is derived from Gewissae, an Irish tribe who claimed descent from Carausius and Casnar Wledig (see Walk 24 Portchester). Cerdic is a British name, similar to Ceredig and Caradoc. He was the son of Elesa, son of Esla, who are recorded on the Pillar of Eliseg near Llangollen in north Wales. Elesa, or Elasius, welcomed St Germanus, Bishop of Auxerre, in 447, so he must have been on the side of the papacy in its campaign against the Pelagian heretics, with their Druid ideas on reincarnation and the law of cause and effect, rather than obedience to Rome .

Religion and the question of whether Britain should build a robust independent state or seek to remain part of the old Roman world seem to have coloured local territorial disputes. Elesa (and Cerdic) seem to have been expelled from Powys around 465, when Ambrosius overthrew Vortigern, the tyrant who had gained power with the help of the Saxons whom he invited to settle in Kent. Cerdic spent his exile in the Lower Loire region of France (the Nantes – Angers area) before returning to regain his lost territory in what is now Hampshire with the aid of the Saxon federates with whom he got on so well. Clearly this little corner of the country has seen its dramatic moments, most of which are still shrouded in mystery.

## The Walk

1.  With your back to Whitefield Farm (no 38 bus terminus, Langley), go left along the road until there is a sign-posted bridleway on your right (also part of the Hampshire County Council Off Road Cycle Trail). Go right along this path and pass East Hill Farm on your left, having ignored a sign-posted path going left just before it.

2.  Go ahead along the farm access track. Ignore a waymarked path forking right. Bear left with the track to reach a road. Cross the road to take the sign-posted footpath opposite. Walk along the left-hand edge of a field and past woodland on

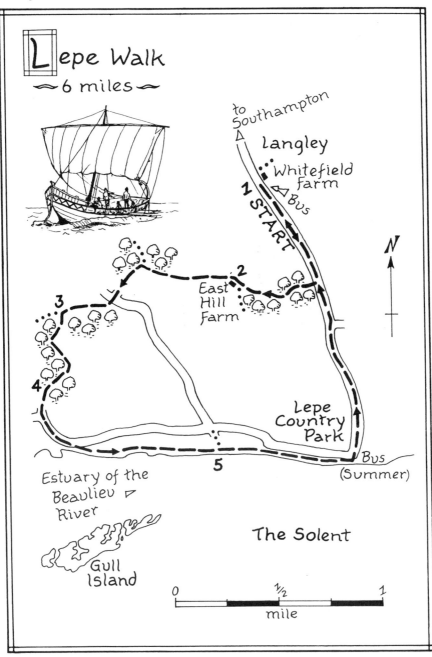

# Lepe Walk
## ~ 6 miles ~

to Southampton
Langley
Whitefield Farm
Bus
1 START

2
East Hill Farm

3

4

Lepe Country Park

Bus (Summer)

5

Estuary of the Beaulieu River

Gull Island

The Solent

N

0        ½        1
mile

your left. Continue past an open field on your left and reach a sign-posted path junction at the start of more woodland.

3. Turn left to walk with the woodland on your right. Keep to the right-hand edge of two fields, go ahead over a stile and turn left in the next corner to reach a signpost where the hedge turns right. Go right for 200 metres, then bear right over a footbridge next to a signpost. Bear left to reach another footbridge, cross it and continue to a signpost.

4. Bear left to reach a road. Go left towards the Solent. Look for a stile and a signpost on your right. The right of way along the shore here is liable to flooding at high tide, so if in doubt, continue along the road to Lepe. If able to take the sign-posted path, cross the stile and walk with the sea on your right.

5. Pass a path going inland on your left. Continue with the sea on your right. Join the road at Lepe Country Park and go inland with the road when it bears left back to the bus terminus.

## Also of Interest:

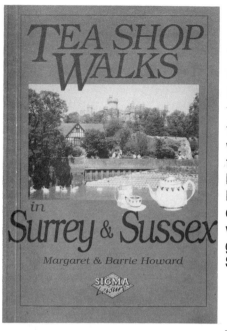

### TEA SHOP WALKS IN SURREY AND SUSSEX

*Margaret and Barrie Howard*

This popular book caters for a market that has previously been neglected by walking guides, yet it contains many fascinating historical sites. Written by husband and wife team Margaret and Barrie Howard, this book of walks will open the eyes of both locals and visitors to the splendid tea-rooms and good walking to be had in Surrey and Sussex. £6.95

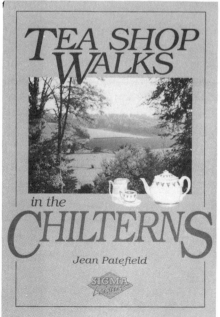

### TEA SHOP WALKS IN THE CHILTERNS

*Jean Patefield*

This perennial favourite is the perfect introduction to walking the Chilterns — and discovering the tea shops! £6.95

### TEA SHOP WALKS IN HAMPSHIRE ˙

*Margaret and Barrie Howard*

With walks in the New Forest, the Isle of Wight and all of Hampshire's beauty spots, this new book will delight tea shop fans in the region. The Howards have sought out the best cafes and created an interesting and rewarding walk to accompany a visit there, making sure your feet and your taste buds are in for a treat! £6.95

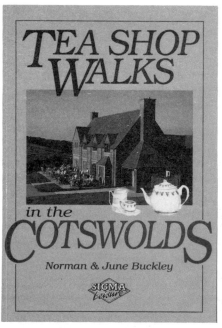

## TEA SHOP WALKS IN THE COTSWOLDS

*Norman & June Buckley*

No other area in Britain has as many tea shops as the Cotswolds. This book of 26 walks takes the reader the length and breadth of the area, visiting the popular towns and tiny villages. Walks average 5-6 miles and each features a tea shop that welcomes walkers. *£6.95*

## TEA SHOP WALKS IN SHROPSHIRE

*Julie Meech*

Shropshire is perfect for both walking and tea shops, so it's a perfect addition to our series! Photographer and writer Julie Meech has walked many miles, drunk many cups of tea and devoured dozens of scones to discover the perfect combinations: easy-going walks, with much to enjoy – all with the reward of a Shropshire tea shop. *£6.95*

## DOGS' LONDON: The City's Best Walks for Dogs and their Owners

*Mary Scott*

20 walks for London's dogs and their owners, all beginning and ending at tube or BR stations. Each walk contains unrestricted runs for dogs: and pleasant, green scenery for their human companions! Information on pubs and open-air cafés where people can eat and drink with a dog in tow. Illustrated with maps and original cartoons, the walks have been tested by Mary and her dog, Fred.　*£6.95*

## RAILWAY RAMBLES: London & South-East

*Clive Higgs*

Londoner Clive Higgs has never owned a car and has accumulated a lifetime's knowledge of London's trains and country walking - "Get down to the booking office now" FARNHAM HERALD. £4.95

## LONDON BUS-TOP TOURIST

*John Wittich*

This book shows where the tourist spots are, where to get off the bus to visit them and how to explore on foot. It covers 10 bus routes, chosen to show a cross-section of London and is designed to make the most of a tourist's time. Written by a well-known guide and lecturer with the London Tourist Board. £6.95

## A YEAR OF WALKS: Sussex

*Roy Woodcock*

This book of 12 circular walks, one for each month of the year, visits a range of outstanding locations in Sussex and provides both half-day and full-day walks in each place. The month-by-month approach allows the countryside to be appreciated through the changing seasons, and means walking doesn't have to be restricted to the summer. Especially suitable to locals, this book will give a new experience and insight to this popular region which contains two Areas of Outstanding Natural Beauty. £6.95

## BY-WAY BIKING IN THE CHILTERNS

*Henry Tindell*

The Chilterns is a popular area for cyclists of all abilities and this book describes a wide variety of routes on all types of terrain. Routes follow quiet lanes and off-road tracks. £6.95

## CYCLING IN & AROUND BIRMINGHAM

*Philip Routledge*

This book guides the cyclist to the very best cycling opportunities around Birmingham and covers an immense variation of landscape, townscape and dedicated cycle routes. £6.95

All of our books are available from your local bookshop. In case of difficulty, or to obtain our complete catalogue, please contact:

**Sigma Leisure, 1 South Oak Lane, Wilmslow, Cheshire SK9 6AR**
**Phone: 01625-531035**
**Fax: 01625-536800**
**E-mail:**
**sigma.press@zetnet.co.uk**

ACCESS and VISA orders welcome. Please add £2 p&p to all orders.